PRESIDENT COOLIDGE

A Contemporary Estimate

Photograph by Havelock Pierce

PRESIDENT COOLIDGE

A CONTEMPORARY ESTIMATE

BY

EDWARD ELWELL WHITING

The ATLANTIC MONTHLY PRESS
BOSTON

FOREWORD

In the spring of 1920 Calvin Coolidge was under consideration as a candidate for the Republican nomination for the presidency. An organization in behalf of this candidacy had begun operations when Governor Coolidge issued a formal statement saying that he was not a candidate. He did so because he regarded it as not proper for the Governor of Massachusetts to enter a contest for delegates. This statement by him placed those advocating his nomination in a difficult position. The movement to nominate him continued, but without his consent, and without any consultation with him thereafter.

When the delegates and others arrived in Chicago in June for the Republican National Convention, one of his friends undertook to draw from Mr. Coolidge a statement which might be helpful. He drafted a telegram thus : —

"Your friends here all send their best wishes and want to know if you are a candidate. What shall I tell them?"

He believed this telegram would produce an interesting reply. It did. The reply was this : —

"Thank my friends for their good wishes and tell them the truth."

It is in accord with the spirit of the Governor's telegram on that occasion that this book is written : "Tell them the truth."

E. E. W.

October 15, 1923

CONTENTS

CONTENTS

CHRONOLOGY

1872 July 4. *Born at Plymouth, Vermont.*

"I love the hills."

1880–1891 *At School.*

"Civilization depends not only upon the knowledge of the people, but upon the use they make of it. If knowledge be wrongfully used, civilization commits suicide. . . . Education must give not only power but direction. It must minister to the whole man or it fails."

1885 March 14. *Death of mother, Victoria Josephine Moor Coolidge.*

"Reverence is the measure not of others but of ourselves."

1891–1895 *Amherst College.*

"The individual may not require the higher institutions of learning, but society does. Without them civilization as we know it would fall from mankind in a night. They minister not alone to their own students, they minister to all humanity."

1895–1897 *Studying law.*

"It may be of little importance to determine at any

time just where we are, but it is of the utmost importance to determine whither we are going. Set
the course aright and time must bring mankind to
the ultimate goal."

1897   June 29. *Admitted to the bar*.

"Courts are established not to determine the popularity of a cause, but to adjudicate and enforce
rights."

1899   *Northampton City Council. Enters politics.*

"Politics is not an end, but a means. It is not a
product, but a process. It is the art of government.
Like other values it has its counterfeits. So much
emphasis has been placed upon the false that the
significance of the true has been obscured and politics has come to convey the meaning of crafty
and cunning selfishness, instead of candid and sin-
cere service. The Greek definition shows a nobler
purpose. *Politikos* means city-rearing, statecraft.
And when we remember that city also meant civilization, the spurious presentment, mean and
sordid, drops away and the real figure of the politician, dignified and honorable, a minister to civilization, author and finisher of government, is
revealed in its true and dignified proportions."

1900–1901   *City Solicitor, Northampton.*

"Office-holding is the incidental, but the standard of
citizenship is the essential. Government does rest
upon the opinions of men. Its results rest on their
actions. This makes every man a politician
whether he will or no. This lays the burden on
us all."

1903   *Clerk of Courts, Hampshire County, Massachusetts.*

"We need more of the office desk and less of the show-window in politics. Let men in office substitute the midnight oil for the limelight."

1905   October 4. *Married Miss Grace Goodhue of Burlington, Vermont.*

1907–1908   *Massachusetts House of Representatives.*

"Men do not make laws. They do but discover them. Laws must be justified by something more than the will of the majority. They must rest on the eternal foundation of righteousness. That state is most fortunate in its government which has the aptest instruments for the discovery of laws. The latest, most modern, and nearest perfect system that statesmanship has devised is representative government. Its weakness is the weakness of us imperfect human beings who administer it. Its strength is that even such administration secures to the people more blessings than any other system ever produced. No nation has discarded it and retained liberty."

1910–1911   *Mayor of Northampton.*

"We may need new charters, new constitutions, and new laws at times. We must always have an alert and interested citizenship. We have no dependence but the individual. New charters cannot save us. They may appear to help us but the chances are

that the beneficial results obtained come from an
increased interest aroused by discussing changes.
Laws do not make reforms, reforms make laws.
We cannot look to government. We must look to
ourselves.''

1912–1915   *Massachusetts State Senate.*

"The people cannot look to legislation generally for
success. Industry, thrift, character, are not conferred by act or resolve. Government cannot relieve
from toil. It can provide no substitute for the rewards of service. . . . Self-government means
self-support.''

1914   *President of the Massachusetts State Senate.*

"Have faith in Massachusetts. In some unimportant
detail some other states may surpass her, but in
the general results there is no place on earth where
the people secure, in a larger measure, the blessings of organized government, and nowhere can
those functions more properly be termed self-
government.''

1915   January 6. *Again President of the Mas-
       sachusetts State Senate.*

ENTIRE SECOND INAUGURAL ADDRESS

"Honorable Senators: — My sincerest thanks I
offer you. Conserve the firm foundations of our
institutions. Do your work with the spirit of
a soldier in the public service. Be loyal to the
Commonwealth and to yourselves. And be brief;
above all things, be brief.''

1916–1918 *Lieutenant-Governor of Massachusetts.*

"I am not one of those who believe votes are to be won by misrepresentations, skillful presentations of half-truths, and plausible deductions from false premises. Good government cannot be found on the bargain counter."

1919–1920 *Governor of Massachusetts.*

"It is your duty not only to reflect public opinion but to lead it. Whether we are to enter a new era in Massachusetts depends upon you. The lessons of the war are plain. Can we carry them into peace? Can we still act on the principle that there is no sacrifice too great to maintain the right? Shall we continue to advocate and practise thrift and industry? Shall we require unswerving loyalty to our country? These are the foundations of all greatness." (From inaugural address to the Legislature.)

1919 November. *Mentioned for presidential nomination.*

"The time requires of men charged with public responsibility a singleness of purpose. The curse of the present is the almost universal grasping for power in high places and in low, to the exclusion of the discharge of obligations. It is always well for men to walk humbly."

1920 January 2. *Declines to enter contest for delegates.*

"I have taken no position in which I need to

withdraw. I do not wish to embarrass anyone. I have a great desire to walk humbly and discharge my obligations. My paramount obligation is not to expose the great office of Governor, but to guard and protect it. The people are entitled to know that their office is to be administered not for my benefit but for their benefit, and that I am not placing myself in any position where any other object could be inferred. There must be no imputation, however unfounded, that I permit their office to be used anywhere for manipulated purposes. I cannot consent to have their office taken into any contest for delegates in my own state. I have not been and I am not a candidate for President."

June 12. *Nominated for Vice-President by Republican Party.*

"I do not feel that there is any more obligation to run for office than there is to become a banker, a merchant, a teacher, or enter any other special occupation. . . . Some men have a particular aptitude in this direction and some have none. Of course experience counts here as in any other human activity, and all experience worth the name is the result of application, of time and thought and study and practice. If the individual finds he has liking and capacity for this work, he will involuntarily find himself engaged in it. There is no catalogue of such a capacity."

1921 March 4. *Vice-President of the United States.*

"Why some men succeed in public life and others

fail would be as difficult to tell as why some succeed and others fail in other activities. Very few
men in America have started out with any fixed
idea of entering public life, fewer still would ad-
mit having such an idea. . . . This may be in
part due to a general profession of holding to the
principle of Benjamin Franklin that office should
neither be sought nor refused, and in part to the
American idea that the people choose their own
officers, so that public service is not optional."

1923   August 2.   *President of the United States.*

"Of course we look to the past for inspiration, but
inspiration is not enough. We must have action.
Action can only come from ourselves; society,
government, the state, call it what you will, cannot act; our only strength, our only security, lies
in the individual. American institutions are
builded on that foundation. That is the meaning of
self-government, the worth and the responsibility
of the individual. In that America has put all her
trust. If that fail, democracy fails, freedom is a
delusion, and slavery must prevail."

PRESIDENT COOLIDGE

I

EARLY YEARS IN VERMONT

CIRCUMSTANCES often raise men to high place. Circumstances do not make men; they give them opportunities. Calvin Coolidge has been raised to the highest place in the government of our country; circumstances have made this possible; it was the man himself, and not circumstance, that translated opportunity into achievement and evolved from the country boy of Vermont a strong national figure. The ultimate place of this man in history is yet to be determined. The record of his public service up to this time, when he has stepped into the office made vacant by the death of President Harding, is such as to warrant high expectations. As President of the nation he faces more complex problems, scattered over a wider field, than have come before him hitherto in his career. No one can forecast with precision what any man will do with problems yet unmet. The confidence in Mr. Coolidge's ability and the expectation that as President he will become a figure of distinction in history are based not only upon the detailed record of what he has done in public life, but upon certain qualities of character and a certain attitude of mind which have distinguished him throughout the years of his public service. The foundations of his character and the inclination of his mind are traceable back to the days of his upbringing and early training among sturdy people in a simple, wholesome, and stimulating environment. We find the explanation of Coolidge the man in Coolidge the boy.

Few men whose records are written for the public to read have had a more consistent self-development. One finds in him to-day countless echoes of the voices that spoke to him amid the hills of Vermont, where in his days of boyhood he crystallized and made permanent strong qualities inherited from vigorous stock and favored by environment.

Calvin Coolidge — christened John Calvin Coolidge — was born July 4, 1872, in a little cottage at Plymouth, Vermont. Seekers of "omens" profess to find one in this fact. Yet many men have risen to positions of eminence lacking such an auspicious birthday; and there must be many who remain obscure despite the fact that their birthdays fall upon Independence Day. The omen-seekers find further delight in the fact that when Mr. Coolidge was nominated as the Republican candidate for Vice-President, and when he was elected to that office in 1920, he was forty-eight years old — one year for each State in the Union, or, in more telling phrase, each star of the flag. They may continue this interesting process by observing that, should he be elected President in 1924, he would, at the time of his inauguration, March 4, 1925, be fifty-two years old; the coincidence is that when Abraham Lincoln was inaugurated on March 4, 1861, he also was fifty-two.

Calvin Coolidge has been called "a second Lincoln." He is not. There is no second Lincoln. Abraham Lincoln was distinctively an individual. He was cast in no mould. His place in history is secure and unique. If Mr. Coolidge, by his keen common-sense and his accurate perceptions, recalls in any way the figure of Lincoln, that is as far as the suggestion can carry. Lincoln earned his education against difficulties, acquired knowledge, with wisdom, by determination and persistency, and so hewed out a character and a career by means of prodigious effort. His early days were marked by a frugality close kin to poverty. Calvin Coolidge, like Lincoln, was born in a small house in the country. The similarity of their conditions stops there. The boyhood of Calvin Coolidge was marked by the sane frugality characteristic of New England life; but there was no touch of poverty in it.

One more curious reminiscence concerning the earliest days of Coolidge may as well be recorded. Seekers of omens may find comfort in this paragraph. His mother's name was Victoria Josephine; both are names of queens. It is recalled by old-timers in Plymouth that even on the day of his birth some of the neighbors said, in view of this fact, and in view of the fact that he was born on Independence Day, he would inevitably become President of the United States! This engaging anecdote — or reminiscence — is not here set down as having the dignity of prophecy. It is the obvious prognostication which must be made and almost invariably is made by those who read the signs on the birthday of any child. If every child for whom the presidency of the United States has been prophesied were to fill that office, most of the country would live in the White House at the same time.

The boy's father was — and is — a man of character and substance, a typical New England man of the kind bred in the hills. Colonel John Coolidge, who holds his title through appointment years ago on the staff of Governor Stickney of Vermont, is a farmer who has earned a good living from his farm, who has in past years operated a country store, who has served his state with distinction. He brought up his son in a good home, in which there was comfort, a fine morality, but no luxury.

One is moved to puzzle over the operations of chance in the careers of men. The American ancestors of Calvin Coolidge settled at Watertown, Massachusetts, in 1630. Why did they leave Massachusetts and go into the Vermont wilderness? Why did they select the remote region which is now Plymouth Notch, fourteen hundred feet above sea level and — in the days when the Coolidges came there — a wild and difficult country? No one knows. Calvin Coolidge's father has been asked why his ancestors settled there. He says it is probable that when some members of the family marched through those hills in the Revolutionary army, to join Ethan Allen, they took a fancy to the country; being of pioneer stock, driven by that quality which settled early America, they chose the place, possibly for its beauty, possibly because they saw there opportunities for home-making and prosperity in a virgin land. One might speculate endlessly and fruitlessly on what would have been the course of the family history had they remained near the place where they settled and so developed future generations under the influence of life near a large city, instead of in the environment of the Vermont hills. Tracing back the authority of fate is futile though fascinating. Whether Calvin Coolidge, born in a suburb of Boston, would have been the same man as the one we know, product of a Vermont farm, no one can say. Thus chance claims its share in the history of men and nations.

The boy received his early education in the district school of the village. In other hours he worked on his father's farm, or on the adjoining farm of a relative. In other words, he led the kind of life known to thousands of American boys born and brought up in country villages. Plymouth contains a church, a store, a small cheese-factory, a district school, and about half a dozen houses. It lies in a little pocket in the hills twelve miles from Ludlow, a prosperous manufacturing town on the railroad.

In such towns there is no luxury and no poverty. The land yields a good living to him who tills it. The scene about the home in which Calvin Coolidge grew up included the village street, which is a country road, houses set back at a little distance across sloping fore-yards, slanting fields of mowing-land framed by forests in which maple trees are predominant, and rising at one side of the village, Saltash Mountain — a hill of no great height but of that strong contour which suggests eternal things. The sounds familiar to the boy's ears were those common to such scenes of peace. He heard the birds and the uncounted sounds that contradict the silence we associate with far places; the breeze from the hills was music stirring the imagination which is every boy's birthright. His feet trod the soft earth of roadway and pasture. In those years of life in which we receive lasting impressions, in which character is formed and developed, he lived close to the things which are eternally true. He was responsive to an unusual degree to his environment. He worked hard on the farm, studied his lessons in the little schoolhouse as a normal boy does, and grew toward manhood well equipped with a sense of proportion and a deep-seated veneration for the works of God.

A visitor at the Coolidge home at Plymouth in the spring of 1920, when Calvin Coolidge was under consideration as a possible candidate for the presidency, asked Colonel John about Calvin as a boy on the farm: Was he a good worker? The father was silent. At last he said: "It always seemed to me that Calvin could get more sap out of a maple tree than any of the other boys around here."

Much has been said and written of President Coolidge's thrift in words. The quality is so unusual, particularly among men in politics, that it has constituted something of a mystery in many minds. It is no mystery to those who know the country regions or the stock from which he came. Folks who live in the hill towns incline to silence. Neighbors are not many, and life is not garrulous. There is something like awe always present in the atmosphere of wooded hills. In place of human conversation those who live in such places hear the whispering of winds and the singing of brooks. It is a region for contemplation and quiet. Men brought up from boyhood amid such surroundings often carry with them through life the silence which was cousin to their birthright. Contact with the world of work sometimes breaks in upon and destroys this habit of silence, but not always. Calvin Coolidge is an example of those who carry far afield with them the silent ways in which they were bred.

The visitor at the Plymouth home in 1920 had been trying for half an hour to stimulate the flow of conversation from Colonel John Coolidge. The Colonel was called from the room a moment, and as he closed the door behind him, a woman who was present in the room held up her hands and said to the visitor: "Calvin Coolidge is a chatterer compared with this man."

So much for the older generation of Coolidges.

After Calvin Coolidge took office as President, following the death of President Harding, one of his sons continued to work in a New England tobacco-field. Another boy in the field said to him,—

"Gee! If my father was President of the United States I would n't be working here."

"You would," said young Coolidge, "if your father were my father."

So much for the coming generation.

The Coolidges do not waste words. The brevity and compactness of speech of Calvin Coolidge, developed by the environment of his youth, were inherited from his father and his father's father. It appears likely to be passed on to his sons.

The boyhood of Calvin Coolidge in Vermont was a determining period in his career. It is significant and important — not for any events which occurred there and then, not for any detailed things done or particular lessons learned in the village school, but rather for that indefinable subtle influence which comes into men's lives in early years, guides their thoughts, and shapes their natures toward ends unforeseen but mighty in possibility. It is not easy to say, when one traces back to the beginnings of men's careers, what most influenced them and what operated most to turn them in the direction they subsequently took. It is not easy to say what are the great items in the records of human boyhood. The undefined, unspecific factors are often the vital ones. It is so in the case of Calvin Coolidge. Many boys start life under similar circumstances. There was something in his nature which reacted to them and produced the man now commanding the interest of this nation and all nations.

The effect of the boy's environment remains in the man. He has never lost his love for the hills, nor has he lost the characteristics which

belong to those living among them. A caller
at his office in the State House during his governorship once asked him : "Do you ever think
that you would like some day to return to
Plymouth to live?"

Governor Coolidge was silent for a few moments. Then he said, "I love the hills."

Calvin Coolidge goes back to Plymouth for
his periods of rest. It was there the tragic
news of President Harding's death found him.
He was with his father, living the life of youth
sustained in the environment which had developed the boy into the man. It is there that he
has always been when he has sought quiet and
new strength. He will not go back to Plymouth
to live. His life is cast in greater human fields.
He has been thrown into the world of mighty
events. In them he is a factor. Through all
the years since his boyhood he has been going
in the one direction. Strong men do not retrace
such steps. But to Plymouth he will return
year after year, first, because sentiment draws
him there, and second, because for him there

is more inspiration, more revitalization, more clarifying of vision, more readjustment of proportions in the communion of such a place than in any other corner of the earth. It is important to understand the strong influence of the Plymouth country upon this boy and man. It is important because it gives one of the keys to his character; because it makes understandable the traits of his nature which sometimes have puzzled those unfamiliar with such towns; because the country now has in the White House a transplanting of the high ideals, sane frugality, conscience, and strength which are at once the characteristic and the product of such surroundings.

If the Plymouth upbringing has been important to him personally, it is no less important now to the nation. Vermont shaped Coolidge. Something of its character will now shape the nation. What will be the far-reaching effects of exalting to the highest office in the land such a man, bringing with him such memories and such a flavor of pioneer America, no one can safely prophesy. His countrymen expect great things. The background of Coolidge is good.

The environment and circumstances of his boyhood developed his character. They did not create it. That upon which surroundings worked was given him by his parents and their forbears. No one can look upon the picture of his mother without being impressed by the strength of character in her face. The contour of the forehead, the width between the eyes, the straight look with its suggestion of seriousness — tinged perhaps with melancholy — indicate thoughtfulness, kindness, and an inexorable understanding of right. This picture of his mother stood upon his desk when he was Governor of Massachusetts. It stood upon the desk in the room he occupied as temporary headquarters in the Willard Hotel at Washington in the days immediately following the death of President Harding. It stands upon his desk in the White House now. His mother's name was Victoria Josephine (Moor) Coolidge; she died in 1885.

His father married again, Carrie (Brown) Coolidge, who died in 1920. His stepmother was as devoted to him as a mother to a son. She died after a painful illness. Her last days were made beautiful by the happiness she found in the new honors given to him. He had been nominated a candidate for Vice-President of the United States. She had no doubt of his election. She had no doubt of anything concerning his future.

One day in the spring of 1920 a visitor sat in the living-room of the Coolidge home in Plymouth. Upon the wall hung a large framed portrait of Calvin Coolidge. Beneath it, upon a couch, lay Mrs. Coolidge. She was very ill. At her side sat a nurse. She had asked to be brought into the room in order that she might hear the conversation about her son. For a few moments the visitor was alone with Mrs. Coolidge and the nurse. Mrs. Coolidge said, "I suppose Calvin is a very busy man."

The caller agreed that he was. Mrs. Coolidge continued: "I want to tell you something about him. No mother ever had a better son than Calvin has been to me—and you know I am not his own mother. Never a week goes by without a letter from him. Often he writes two or three times a week. I do not believe many boys write to their mothers like that."

Mothers who love their sons are fortunate to have sons who understand.

It has been indicated on an earlier page that Calvin Coolidge inherits his gift of brevity of speech from his father and his grandfather. He inherits from them much more. John C. Coolidge, rugged, tall, erect, strong-featured, and silent, has the appearance of a man hewn from the very rocks of his home state. He is well along in years, but there is about him little suggestion of age. His is the breed which grows straight and stays strong. His features are large and speak of sturdy stock. It was from such men as he that the perseverance and vigor came to establish on these shores a new race. He has been a useful citizen all his life. He has served his State in the legislature, has been a constable of his town, and a friend and associate of men effective in large fields. He is and always has been a farmer; there is nothing in his appearance or his life to suggest the bent-backed, whiskered ignorance of the comic-paper farmer. His eye is shrewd and kindly. Into it frequently comes a twinkle, for he has the dry sense of humor of his kind.

Men of this sort have in their hearts all the wealth of sentiment and emotion. They control them with a firm will. This reticence of father and son is instinctive and inbred; that its cultivation by a cautious man may give value to the man and to the causes he serves is obviously true. Calvin Coolidge has so cultivated this quality. Public men have often found cautiousness of utterance an asset.

Calvin's life as a boy on his father's farm was like that of most boys similarly placed. He worked hard and liked it. "He was a great hand on the farm," says his father. There were no strict rules of conduct. "If there are rules," Colonel Coolidge once said to a friend, "it gives a boy a chance to break them. I told Calvin always to do his job well, and he always did. That 's what my father taught me, and that's what his father taught him.''

On July 4, 1920, his forty-eighth birthday anniversary, Calvin, then Republican candidate for Vice-President, arrived in Plymouth, Vermont, for a rest preceding the campaign. He drove up to his father's house, alighted from the car, and shook his father's hand. Colonel John put his hand on his son's shoulder and said, ''Hello, Cal!'' That was all the formality of the home-coming of a son who had stepped well forward on the path of great achievement.

Colonel Coolidge thoroughly understands his boy. He put his finger on the key of his son's career when he said, ''He did fairly well as Governor and I guess he 'll do fairly well as President.'' Calvin as a boy learned on his father's farm the value of the lesson that it was worth while to do to the best of his ability the thing immediately at hand. The fruit of this training is seen throughout his career.

He is not disposed to grapple with problems which are not within the range of his immediate concern. He was taught as a boy to be ready for, but not to anticipate, tasks to be done. Mark Sullivan tells a story of Coolidge which may serve to illustrate this. When the League of Nations first became an issue Mr. Coolidge was Governor of Massachusetts. Mr. Sullivan, as a writer, asked him what he thought of the League. Governor Coolidge's reply was immediate, and it was this: —

"I am the Governor of Massachusetts. The State of Massachusetts has no foreign relations. If ever I should hold an office calling for action or opinion on this subject, I shall put my mind on it and try to arrive at the soundest conclusions within my capacity."

The President's boyhood and youth on a farm, and the fact that his father and those before him were farmers, become now of national importance. The most acutely disturbing problem before the national government, in both its executive and legislative branches, is that of agriculture. It is an intricate problem. Solution has been sought by direct methods which do not serve. The task of establishing this basic occupation on a foundation so firm that it will prosper as it should for the national welfare is not to be achieved by any simple process of one-track legislation. It is comparatively easy for Congress to enact a law improving the financial credit of farmers. It is comparatively easy to enact a law guaranteeing the prices of farm products. Other specifics for the cure of agricultural distress have been offered and applied. They have not solved the problem. The demand has come for special Congressional sessions and for other particular efforts to meet and assuage economic unrest in the farming districts of the country. There is no mistaking the sincerity and earnestness of the demand for effective treatment of this real national problem. To chart a way which shall lead to permanently good results, to avoid the reefs and shallows of futile or pernicious legislation, to distinguish between quack panaceas and true treatment, calls for leadership of a high order. It calls also for a sympathetic understanding, in such leadership, of the trials, difficulties, and hopes of men who till the soil.

It seems peculiarly fortunate in this crisis of national affairs that Calvin Coolidge, now President, should first trace his origin and his early training to the farm; second, that he should have had long and thorough training in legislative and executive experience; third, that he should have retained and cherished throughout all his years of public life, a keen appreciation of and love for those things which concern the farmer.

From a Vermont farm, a boy reared under the best traditions of rural life has traveled over the road of experience into national leadership. He has carried with him memories of his youth. He has kept in contact with the scenes which were his as a boy. Thus we find now in the office of President of the United States, a "dirt farmer" who has joined to his feeling for the needs of the worker of the soil a highly developed knowledge of the ways by which desirable ends may best be attained. It is not likely that President Coolidge has a perfected plan for the immediate solution of the great problem of American agriculture. It is certain that he has an understanding sympathy with those who demand relief. It is certain that he has a technical command of the processes by which solution of this problem can be approached. It is certain that he will be a listener to those who have wise suggestions. It is certain, furthermore, that during his term in the presidency progress will be made toward the establishment of agriculture in its proper place as an industry and as a bulwark of American independence. Into what paths and byways this may beckon Congress, by what routes consummation of the purpose shall ultimately be sought, no man knows.

"The boy is father to the man." In no case of a public man in our time has the importance of boyhood environment and training, or the importance of ancestral stock, been more significant than in the case of Calvin Coolidge. This is so because that boyhood was strongly marked and because the grown man has never loosened his hold upon the lessons and the principles then given him. Traits early developed find manifestation now. We have as President a trained public man of considerable experience. We have something besides; it reaches back to the very foundation of the Republic. We have the conscience of the best that is in New England. We have a personification of basic American principles: thrift, caution, courage, balance, and a keen sense of what is right. What this will produce is for time to show.

II

AT SCHOOL AND COLLEGE

CALVIN COOLIDGE received his first book-education in the Plymouth Notch district school. "Plymouth Notch" is the local name for that section of the town in which the Coolidges live; the other village in the town is called Plymouth Union. The school building in which Calvin learned to read and write is no longer standing. A new but no larger building is on its site. It was what is commonly called a typical New England school. It is less typical than it used to be. The old-fashioned district school has been much celebrated in sentiment and memory. It usually was presided over by a teacher, man or woman, who taught within the limits of his or her knowledge a miscellaneous group of boys and girls from primary to high-school age. The character of these schools varied according to the nature of the population and the remoteness of the district. Where the school was fortunate in its choice of teachers it sometimes provided that rare type of fine education which consisted rather of a training of character than of instruction in details. The school at Plymouth Notch was a good school of its kind.

What pictures we sometimes get of the boyhood of men who have become famous! A campaign leaflet concerning Coolidge gives us the crushing information that "he has never played, boy or man — marbles, baseball, golf, anything. His only avocations have been the gratification of an almost instinctive philosophical sense with the best books, a love of nature, and walking." This is a melancholy picture. We should not like to think it is correct. It is scant justice to any man to picture his boyhood as consisting of social isolation and introspection. This boy, as a matter of fact, was like any normal boy. He did have a serious bent of mind, and he did work hard. He minded his father, did his duty as a farmer's son, learned his lessons, and, in fact, was a pretty good youngster. He was not a freak.

What father has not stories of the precocity of his child? These stories often are dull; but they cease to be dull if the precocious child later achieves fame. Here is a story emphasizing the retentive memory of Calvin Coolidge at a tender age. Colonel Coolidge took the boy, when he was two years old, to the State House at Montpelier. Thirty-six years later, Calvin visited that State House for the first time since he had been there as a two-year-old. On this later occasion, as he walked into the building with his father he stopped, looked at an empty corner, and said: "They 've moved the catamount, have n't they?" The father remembered then that years ago a stuffed catamount had stood in that now empty corner.

This anecdote of Coolidge's very early youth may be taken to prove — not that he was an unusual boy, but that he was quite normal, though possibly his memory was a little more retentive than that of most children. The story of Coolidge and the catamount at Montpelier is no great evidence of exceptional mental power on his part, but it will serve the far better purpose of showing that he was normally observant and a fair average boy.

In the district school of Plymouth, Calvin was as fond of pranks and as addicted to plaguing the teacher as any boy would be. On top of the school stove was an iron image, supposed to be an ornament. The boys in the school found much joy in shooting wads of paper at it by means of a lead pencil and a rubber band. Whether Calvin was impressed by the inadequacy of the weapon or was simply impelled by lack of ownership of one himself, it is of record that he manufactured a substitute which was much more powerful. One day in school, behind the shelter of a geography book, he took careful aim at the iron image on the stove and scored a bull's-eye the first shot.

Why is it that as soon as a man becomes eminent his fellow men proceed to create for him a fictitious and usually abnormal past? It is far more stimulating to humanity to feel that the men who rise to heights are not eccentric in every instance; it is a helpful thought that the boy and youth who are like their fellows are not by such normality barred from all possibilities of success. The pages of history carry countless names of odd geniuses who from a curious and unusual youth have developed amazing qualities and so have towered far above the rest of the world and entered the gallery of giants. Such men do not tell the whole story of human events. Men, to have command of the confidence of others, and to undertake and maintain leadership in great causes, need to have a bond of sympathy with their kind. The average boy may have within him certain prosaic qualities which, developed and strengthened, may be applied for the salvation of freedom and for the advancement of civilization.

There was nothing abnormal in the nature of George Washington or of Abraham Lincoln.

Each was essentially human: that is, each possessed the proper balance of admirable human qualities, to which each added a particular strength of character and a particular development of what was in him, and so each became a leader of men. There are many anecdotes of these two great Americans which emphasize early indications of qualities which later became potent in shaping the history of the world. Yet what father has not seen in his son those same qualities? What father has not been puzzled, trying to understand why his son has not received from the world that recognition which he thinks should have been his? It has been said that all the qualities of all humanity are latent in every man. How these qualities may be balanced and how they may be made productive to the advantage of the individual and society, is the problem of all. Modern methods of education and countless social factors grapple with the puzzle, but without the initiative of the individual few can rise.

The boyhood of Calvin Coolidge was not abnormal. There are thousands of boys growing up every year on American farms who are much like him. That he had some strong strain of character which, even in his boyhood, was directing his abilities to purposeful ends, may be true. But we examine the records of his youth, and we consult those who were his acquaintances then, only to find the picture of a boy very like other boys, plus a little more seriousness, and possessing — which is important — a strong sense of duty. "Never once," said his father to a friend, "did I give Calvin a job that he did not finish. I might have gone away and left him with the job to do, but when I came back I always found it done. I never told him twice." On the farm at Plymouth is a small bureau, or chiffonier, which Calvin made as a boy. It is a good job.

There is a story of him when he was a boy at the Plymouth district school, about ten years old. A visitor in the Coolidge house was wakened about two A.M. by the sound of someone

moving about. Thinking possibly that someone was ill, she went downstairs to investigate. In the dark she found the small boy. She
asked him why he was stirring about at such
an hour. He told her, "I forgot to bring in the
firewood. I am going out to get it."

Stories of Coolidge's boyhood are conflict-
ing. On the one hand we hear that he "never
played." On the other, there are plenty of
anecdotes of pranks he played in the Plymouth
school, at Black River Academy, at St. Johnsbury, and at Amherst College. There is a
story of an occasion in the Plymouth district
school when, because of some mischief or
other, young Coolidge was vigorously shaken
by the teacher. The teacher on this occasion
was a man. He shook the boy so vigorously
that some of the buttons were torn from his
coat. The next morning Coolidge came to
school with a handful of buttons and a needle
and thread. The boys asked him what that
meant. His reply was: "He tore 'em off, now
he can sew 'em on again."

It is not on record that the teacher did so.

The truth of the matter presumably is that the Coolidge boy differed little from other boys. He was a quiet boy, of average health and strength, but never of an athletic type. He was thoughtful and he had been brought up under a kindly but firm discipline. It was the sort of discipline common to many American homes of the period, in which physical chastisement played no part, but in which there was no debate on questions of obedience. Boys brought up in such homes do not argue with their parents. An order given, or a task set, presupposes obedience and accomplishment. Thus, whatever of strength there was in the boy's character, whatever of mental vigor, whatever of the powers of concentration and application inherited from his ancestors, were further developed and made dominant in his nature by the simplicity and sanity of his upbringing.

We may now dismiss the discussion of whether or not as a boy he showed startling signs of future eminence. We may dismiss it by once more quoting his father. Someone once asked him what was the secret of his son's success. His reply is quoted thus : "I cannot say that Calvin was an extraordinary boy. I had no thought that he would become a great man. He was a quiet boy. He did what I told him and did it well. But I never thought he was more remarkable than other boys."

Sifting the evidence, then, we find nothing of a prophetic nature in the boyhood of Calvin Coolidge.

The next school attended by young Coolidge, after leaving the district school in Plymouth, was the Black River Academy at Ludlow. This was his first step away from home. It was not a definite severance of connection, however, for he frequently traveled the twelve miles back and forth between Ludlow and Plymouth. He had not lost the home contact. He was standing on the bridge between home and the future. Of his days at Black River, and later at the school in St. Johnsbury, there is little to tell. He took no part in athletic contests, he studied his lessons, and probably lived about as the other boys did in similar circumstances, always, perhaps, being a little more serious-minded than most of his comrades. That his mind was turned toward public life in these years is not especially indicated. He had already attended Plymouth town meetings as a boy, but this presumably was because his father filled the office of moderator. It is not likely that this experience aroused in him con-scious understanding of the foundations of American government. Yet it is altogether likely that his subsequent interest in and understanding of the principles of American representative democracy were in large degree traceable to this early intimate contact with the operations of a process lying at the very base of the American nation. The town meeting is democracy operating in full force. To these meetings come the citizens of the town, fore-warned by the warrant which has been posted, for the inspection of the townsfolk, well in advance of the date of the meeting. Every problem of the town's affairs finds its way into such gatherings.

Properly conducted, these New England meetings are veritable fountains of free speech. Here speaks the early insistent voice of America. Every town meeting has its conservative members, its "standpatters," its reformers, trouble-makers, cranks, and eccentrics. The meeting is a sifting process for all the ideas, ideals, and isms of the countryside. It is the theory of our representative form of government that the spirit of these fundamental American political institutions shall be carried forward in State Legislatures and in Congress, where men chosen to represent their fellow citizens come together and discuss as best they may such problems as in the older and simpler form were directly in the hands of the people who made up the attendance at town meetings. The old meetings were not — and are not — free from the contaminations of sordid and predatory politics. The spoilsman and the

exploiter will always seek their opportunity
under any form of government. None is proof
against them. Eternal vigilance is the price
not only of liberty but of honesty and wisdom
in self-government. We do not know what in-
fluences operated in the town meetings which
Calvin Coolidge attended as a boy; we do
know that at an impressionable age he saw
with his own eyes and heard with his own ears
the machinery of democracy in full and effective operation. It is probable that when he
later determined upon a public career for himself, and when he undertook such a career, some
flavor of his early contact with town government remained to influence his understanding
of the problems of all government.

Although Coolidge was called by his name,
Calvin, in these early days, this was to distinguish him from his father, each being named
John. It was not until about the time of his
graduation from Amherst College in 1895 that
he definitely dropped all use of his first name
and became simply "Calvin Coolidge." The

retention of the names, John and Calvin, in the
Coolidge family has an obvious significance,
marking the rigorous religious background of
the family traditions. (The two Coolidge boys,
sons of the President, are named respectively
John and Calvin.) In the dropping of the name
John, thus shortening the signature to two
names, omen-seekers have one more of their
delightful opportunities. They recall, of course,
that Stephen Grover Cleveland dropped the
"Stephen"; that Thomas Woodrow Wilson
dropped the "Thomas"; that the Father of
his Country was George Washington, and that
the savior of the Union was Abraham Lincoln. Yet there are thousands of men of similarly abbreviated names who do not become
president; and a list of presidents shows many
who use all the names that fancy dictated to
their parents. However, it is true that the
sound of "Calvin Coolidge" has greater political utility than would "John C. Coolidge,"
or "John C. Coolidge, Jr." Whether young
Calvin had any premonition of the political

usefulness of dropping his first name may be doubted.

Coolidge's career at Amherst was marked by studiousness but was not devoid of the usual incidents connected with undergraduate life. Here, as formerly, he was no athlete. His health and physique were good, but were not such as to incline him to physical exercise for its own sake. The true explanation of his abstention from athletics lies, however, in other than physical reasons. His mind as a boy was — as his mind now is — essentially and uncompromisingly practical. There was nothing in his nature which commended to him effort not productive of results having practical worth. It may be ventured as a statement of truth that there is nothing in the psychology of athletic sport which is within the comprehension of Calvin Coolidge. He had no hostility toward athletics and no disapproval of them; they simply did not interest him. A few years ago some one asked him if he ever took part in athletic events at college. "Some," he said.

As he did not seem inclined to elaborate this brief answer, he was pressed further: "What part did you take?"

"I held the stakes, mostly."

Since his advancement in public life, writers have sought to unearth detailed information concerning his college career. Classmates have been probed with questions. Various accounts are given, but the consensus of opinion is that he was a modest youth, and in fact during his first two years at college was hardly known even to his classmates. One of these recalls that it was not until his junior year that he attracted any attention. In that year he suddenly drew the notice of his fellows by the ability he showed in debate. Says one of them, "He was keen, concise, felicitous, and humorous. It was as if a new and gifted man had joined the class."

Another classmate refers to his lack of interest in athletic affairs, noting that Coolidge confined his exercise to walking and to such gymnasium work as was required by college rules. This man also refers to his prowess in debate. "When he had finished," he says, "his audience knew they had heard from one who knew his subject."

The boy's hobby appears to have been books. Presumably these were works on government, economics, law, and history. These are the subjects which consistently have interested him, and which have shaped his character and career.

His college life was not all seriousness. One of his classmates recalls almost the first intimation the class had of his personality, when he made a speech entitled, "Why I Got Stuck." One of the institutions at Amherst in that day was the so-called "plug-hat race." Each contestant wore a shining silk hat and carried a cane. The winners of the race were entertained by seven losers. Calvin was one of the seven. His speech was an explanation of why he failed to win. This is probably the only race he ever lost.

He did his first political work while at

college. W. J. Blair of Chicago tells the story.
He says Coolidge came to his room one night
during his junior year and took him along to
vote for his friend, Deering, who was a candidate for the board of editors of a class book.
"Need I tell you," asks Mr. Blair, "that Deering was elected?"

At the end of the college course there was, as
usual, a compilation of statistics regarding the
young men, and the usual votes concerning the
relative popularity of different individuals in
various fields. On the question as to which
member of the class was likely to become the
most famous, Calvin Coolidge received one
vote. It was cast by his friend, "Ed" Morrow
—as Mr. Dwight W. Morrow was then called.
Morrow himself received most of the other
votes of the class; he is now a prominent
banker, a man of substance and success, who in
all ways has justified his classmates' belief in
him. But he was the only one of his class who
picked Coolidge as the one of them destined
for the highest eminence.

That Coolidge had a sense of humor was recognized by his classmates who chose him "Grove orator." The Grove oration is a humorous affair concerned with the personalities and incidents of the class. Those who recall it say that it was bright, keen, and witty. That he delivered it with the utmost seriousness might go without saying. The judgment of his classmates is that it was a thoroughly successful piece of work.

Coolidge's hair at that period was red. Time has toned down its color, but in those days he formed one of a group of men who became firm friends because of the similarity of the color of their hair. Professor George D. Olds, now president of Amherst College, came to the college as an instructor in the year that Coolidge's class entered; he has been adopted by the class as a member. At the class reunion in 1920 he spoke of his feeling of loneliness during the first days of his presence on the faculty, and he told how he began to pick out individuals in his classes as possible friends. The first he picked out were those who, like himself, had red hair. In the senior-class picture, all the red-haired men stood together in a row.

It was at the 1920 reunion that one of his classmates said to Coolidge, "Cal, no man living reminds me more of Abraham Lincoln than you do." He replied, "Well, Bob, don't you think he 's a pretty good man to follow?"

Coolidge received his A.B. degree cum laude.

During his senior year he entered a contest open to all American colleges and won the first prize with an essay entitled "Principles Underlying the American Revolution." Since his elevation to the presidency this essay, the product of a youth under twenty-three years of age, has been reprinted. It shows a maturity of thought and an absence of crudity unusual in a young man of that age. It might stand as the serious writing of an authority well established as an historian. This essay may fairly be said to be the first considerable manifestation of those solid mental qualities which explain a large portion of his success in public life.

There is a true story concerning this essay and the medal which signified his victory. This story emphasizes an agreeable but unusual human trait. Some months after his graduation, and when he was reading law and earning his living in the office of Hammond and Field, Northampton, one of his employers saw a news item in a paper which said that a medal for the best essay on the principles for which the Revolutionary War was fought had been awarded to Calvin Coolidge. He put the clipping in front of the young man and asked, —

"Is that true?"

Coolidge nodded his head.

"Well, did you get the medal?"

Another nod.

"Where is it?"

Young Coolidge opened a drawer in his desk and showed the medal.

"How long have you had this?"

"Five or six weeks."

"Have you told your father?"

"No. Would you?"

Accounts agree that Calvin Coolidge lived at college about as other boys lived. He was neither poor nor wealthy. His father paid the necessary college bills. Calvin was always properly clothed, and lived comfortably, though frugally. He ate at a boarding-house which was inexpensive but well conducted. There is a story of this boarding-house which is trivial, but may properly be quoted here simply because it emphasizes what ought to be emphasized frequently — that is, that although he was a serious-minded boy, he indulged in the same kind of nonsense that schoolboys have always liked. On the morning of the story the *pièce de résistance* at breakfast was homely hash. Coolidge tucked in his napkin, seized his knife and fork, then suddenly started in consternation as he gazed upon the dish before him.

"Maria!" he called. Maria was the waitress. Maria entered from the kitchen.

"Maria," asked Calvin, "where is the dog?"

"In the kitchen," said the waitress.

"Bring him in," said Calvin.

Maria whistled to the dog, who came in through the kitchen door. He was a large wholesome-looking dog. He wagged his tail, and trotted out of the room again. Calvin resumed his grasp on the fork and began operations on the dish in front of him, saying in a voice of relief, "It's all right, fellows, let's go ahead."

Thus Coolidge's college days were marked by nothing more than might have warranted expectations of a reasonable success in life. We do not find in them any portents or signs either of future greatness or of high political honors. We find in process of establishment during these years of school and college education estimable qualities of strength, a serious attention to duty, self-control, and a growing understanding of the relative importance of things. It might be said that one of the qualities of character and one of the agencies for success is the ability to develop that portion of one's mental equipment which offers most promise of profitable results. This, apparently, is exactly what Calvin Coolidge was doing at school, and particularly in his final years in college. He appears to have been weighing himself. When he left college and stepped into the study and practice of law, he had solidified qualities which he had unconsciously been developing at Plymouth in boyhood. He stepped from college a young man with a serious purpose, a becoming modesty, a liking for hard work, trained in frugality, conscious of the value of results obtained by serious effort — in short, well equipped to enter the first stages on a pathway which might lead ultimately to success. In the study of these early years the significance is that upon a not unusual foundation, and through a process by no means unique, he faced life as many Americans may. What he has done with his opportunity now becomes a matter of importance to the nation.

III

LAW AND POLITICS

THE law is the natural pathway of political advancement. It is not a sure path, nor is it the only one. The cry for "the business man in politics" has been answered by a crop of successful business men who have won distinction in high political places. The increasing voice of business in government is of course the natural development of political life to accord with the development of the nation whose affairs it directs. The authority of business has even exerted itself within the professions, not omitting that of the law. We hear frequent reference to "the law business," and many law offices are conducted more on the lines of a commercial business than on those which mark the old-fashioned law office. This admixture of professional and business life needs to be kept in mind when we consider the development of

American politics. The drift is not all one way. While the legal profession and other professions have taken on some flavor of business methods, the business man of the present day has acquired — and is proud of — what may be called a professional attitude. In this process may be seen the operation of that unifying force which amalgamates a people marching on ways of material success.

The old type of lawyer, such as Daniel Webster, "the only man who ever looked like a cathedral," is not common to-day. Calvin Coolidge is a fair representative of the modern type of lawyer. He has in his make-up probably more of the flavor of the old-time legal type than many of his contemporaries, yet his law practice, which he developed in Northampton before entering politics, was essentially a practice concerned with affairs of business organization. Thus, while selecting law as the field for his work, he entered a gateway leading toward political opportunities. He carried with him and developed an understanding of business problems and business needs. He became a lawyer who was essentially a lawyer, holding his profession in high respect; but he had none of the old-time impatience with business activities.

There is little or nothing to indicate that Mr. Coolidge at this period of his life foresaw for himself a distinguished or even important political career. If he had dreams of a political future, he either kept them to himself — which is probable — or confided them only to those who have never divulged them. We do not find, in searching into his early years, any of those cryptic utterances which sometimes attach themselves to the early records of men who have in later life attained eminence, and which are then interpreted as prophetic. Young Calvin kept his own counsel regarding his ambitions. His immediate concern, after leaving college, was to study law, to gain admittance to the bar, and, presumably, to practise his profession.

Coolidge went at once to Northampton after

leaving college, his father having approved the
choice of his profession. For this work the
young man was to acquire true reverence. In his
choice of the law, who shall say how great was
the strain upon that reverence which his father
had for the traditional occupation of the family — farming? A friend once asked Colonel
Coolidge if he had expected Calvin to follow in
the family footsteps. "Once," said the father,
"I had a hope that Calvin might some day
take my place here. That was a long time ago.
I never asked him to. He understood what I
thought. One day, while he was studying at
college, he came to me and said, 'Father, do
you want me to take your place here on the
farm?' I answered him, 'Do what you think is
best.' He did. And I think," added Colonel
Coolidge, "his judgment was best."

The young man's choice of law as his profession was deliberate, and coolly made. One
feels safe in saying, though without authority
to do so, that if he had followed his natural
desires he would have remained on the Plym-

outh farm. One can hardly doubt that his inclinations were in this direction. His judgment told him that a wiser choice lay elsewhere.

In the year of his graduation from Amherst College, Calvin Coolidge entered the law office of Hammond and Field of Northampton. There he read law while employed by the firm. It is the old-fashioned way of studying the profession. Undoubtedly financial considerations influenced his choice of this method. His father had paid his necessary college bills and was financially able to continue through a lawschool course. Money, however, was not overabundant. The old-fashioned way of reading law in a law office instead of passing through a law school was chosen. There are those who will tell you that many men learn law more thoroughly this way and enter upon the practice of law with a firmer foundation than any law school can give. That is not the general opinion; but it has its adherents. Certainly for some young men the extra difficulties of earning their living and learning law

in the field of its operations this method sup-
plies an incentive and a spur which produce
good results. That Coolidge was an apt and
industrious pupil is indicated by the fact that,
after being twenty months in Hammond and
Field's office, he was admitted to the bar. The
date of his admission was June 29, 1897, just
a few days preceding his twenty-fifth birthday.
The motion for his admission was made by
Henry P. Field, his employer.

By this time he had established with his
employers and with their clients a reputation
for caution, carefulness, thoroughness — and
silence. There is a story of a client who came
into the office one day when Coolidge had not
long been there, seeking consultation with the
head of the firm. Coolidge was the only one in
the office, and with much reluctance the client
discussed the case with him. During the discussion, however, he was so impressed by the
youth's knowledge of law and by the sanity of
his comment, that he later took occasion to tell
Judge Field of the impression made upon him

and to predict a distinguished future for the young man. This anecdote is told merely because it emphasizes a fact which is pertinent to that period of young Coolidge's development. He was not only reading law; he was serving those with whom he was associated. He was applying his knowledge; he was "doing the day's work."

Two qualities, not extraordinary in themselves but powerfully effective when maintained consistently, explain much of Mr. Coolidge's success in politics. These are the quality of cold judgment and the quality of doing the work immediately at hand. Neither of these is a magic attribute of character; each can be developed by almost any person. He began their development young, and he persevered.

There is nothing sensational or dramatic to report regarding Mr. Coolidge's early practice. He did not loom large as a trial lawyer, but his services were much sought as a counselor. His practice was without incident bearing particularly on his future. His reputation was good with his clients and with his fellow lawyers. He became a director and counsel for the Nonotuck Savings Bank in Northampton. He numbered among his clients men and interests of substance and importance. His reputation and personality appealed to the local Republicans as desirable party assets, and he was chosen a member of the Republican city committee, of which he later became chairman. This was his entry into the active political field.

He did not thereafter follow the routine way. Instead of continuing through local and State committees in the machine work of politics, he stepped almost immediately into public office. He was elected in 1899 to the city council of Northampton. He served two terms in this office. Accounts agree that he was a youthful councilman who took his duties seriously. We do not find any record of sensationalism or any dramatic incidents forecasting future events. At the end of his second term he became a candidate for the office of city solicitor and was elected. In this essential-

ly legal office he served with ability. He served
for a time as examiner of titles for Hampshire
County, and in 1903 was appointed to fill an
unexpired term as clerk of courts for that
county. He could have been nominated and
elected for the following term, but he declined.

At this time he became increasingly active
in what may be called practical political work.
He was made chairman of the Republican city
committee. It is of record that he was an efficient chairman, and that the committee under his direction increased its authority and
effectiveness. This period is of importance in
considering his life, because it provided the
first test of his abilities as an organizer and — in
a small way — as a party leader. It is well to
recall this period also in seeking to understand
his precise relation to party politics to-day.
President Coolidge is a firm believer in the
party system of government. The foundation
for that belief, which he has consistently held,
was laid in this preliminary training at Northampton. His conception of party politics

is based upon a belief in the necessity for party responsibility. He is not an intolerant partisan; but he thoroughly believes in the party which he has always served.

At one time during his term as Governor of Massachusetts, a newspaperman, — a Republican,— during a talk with him, recalled whimsically an incident of his own boyhood. He told the story to Governor Coolidge thus : —

"When I was a boy in Springfield, another youngster met me on the street one day and asked me whether I was a Republican or a Democrat. I said I did n't know and asked what difference it made. 'Well,' said the other boy, 'if you are a Democrat you can march in our torchlight parade and come up to my father's flag-raising and have some ice cream.' I replied, 'All right, I 'm a Democrat.' So you see," said the newspaper man to Governor Coolidge, "I sold my first vote to the Democratic Party for a dish of ice cream."

"Well," said the Governor, "you got more than some of the Democrats get."

Yet Calvin Coolidge has always been able to win the support of Democratic voters at the polls. The brief period of leadership of the Northampton Republican city committee presumably strengthened his conviction that effectiveness in government may best be pursued through party responsibility. At least, his subsequent career bears this out. His efforts have been toward party unity because he believes that only so can desired results in government be obtained. Many do not agree with him in this. He is consistent in his belief and in his course. We find instances of his application of this principle often throughout his career. While he was Lieutenant-Governor of Massachusetts he was unreservedly loyal to the Governor. While he was Vice-President of the United States he similarly effaced himself and was heard chiefly as the echo of the President. His critics have alleged that this was evidence of colorlessness and insignificance. Some have translated it as lack of independence. His friends say it is the product of his loyalty,

both to his individual chief and to the party
represented by that chief. It is probably correct to say that the first years of his political
activity impressed upon him the serviceability
as well as the desirability, according to his
viewpoint, of strict party adherence.

It was not as the direct result of his chair-
manship of the city committee, though it was
undoubtedly aided by this service, that he was
nominated as a candidate for the State Legislature, to which he was elected and in which
he began to serve in 1907. His entrance to the
State Legislature is marked by another milestone. He had stepped from the life of Northampton into that of the State capital.

Before we pass this milestone and examine
what is beyond, there is an important event
identified with Northampton to be recorded.
On October 4, 1905, Calvin Coolidge married
Grace A. Goodhue, daughter of Andrew I.
Goodhue of Burlington, Vermont.

This marriage has been utterly happy. There
are two sons, John and Calvin, both of them

PRESIDENT AND MRS. COOLIDGE AND THEIR SONS

now studying at Mercersburg Academy in Pennsylvania. They have been there since their father was elected Vice-President.

In temperament Mrs. Coolidge is almost the opposite of her husband. She has what may be called a keen social consciousness. Her personality is altogether charming; she is invariably popular with all who meet her; she has personal magnetism to an unusual degree: in short, she has all of the social qualities which her husband lacks.

Humorists will not omit to take note of this fact: Grace Goodhue, at the time when she first met Calvin Coolidge, was a teacher in the Clarke School for deaf-mutes, at Northampton.

Mr. Coolidge roomed and boarded with the steward of the Clarke School; Miss Goodhue was a friend of the steward's wife. It was on one evening when she was a guest of her friend at supper that Mr. Coolidge was introduced to her. There are countless stories of their courtship. Most of them are inventions; but some are true. One which has been sanctioned by a person who should know the facts is as follows : —

Mr. Goodhue entered his living-room at Burlington one day and found Calvin Coolidge by himself, reading a magazine. "Hello, Calvin," he said, "what are you doing in Burlington? Come up here on some business?"

"No," said Calvin, "came up to marry Grace."

"Why! Have you spoken to her yet?"

"No; I can wait a few days if it's any convenience to you."

Mrs. Coolidge is blessed with a sense of humor. That there is a humorous side to Calvin Coolidge, both objective and subjective, is undeniable. He has an understanding of humorous things, but it is under perfect control. It is doubtful if he has ever laughed boisterously in his life. His laugh is a chuckle, but he smiles easily and frequently. Though he does not guffaw, he is not unduly solemn. For the rest, any man so celebrated for silence, so redolent of the northern New England flavor, must give rise to many humorous stories. It is at this point that the sense of humor possessed by Mrs. Coolidge enters. She sees in full measure the funny side of life and politics — therefore a story may be told of her husband and herself without offense to either. It concerns the period when Coolidge was Governor of Massachusetts and when they occupied a two-room suite at the Adams House. Mrs. Coolidge had gone to some social gathering in the afternoon; she had left a note for the Governor, giving the telephone number by which she could be reached if necessary. At about five o'clock she was called to the telephone. The conversation was as follows: —

"Is this Grace?"

"Yes."

"This is Cal. Hop home."

Mrs. Coolidge hopped home. The extreme brevity of the message neither offended nor surprised her. She has always understood. She knew that she would not be summoned except for some particular and pressing reason. There was no necessity for details in the telephone conversation. She hurried to the hotel immediately and found that the cause of the summons was adequate.

Mrs. Coolidge is a graduate of the University of Vermont. She was prominent in college affairs, sang in the Glee Club, and was active in dramatic entertainments. They were married at the Goodhue home in Burlington and went to Montreal for a wedding trip; then they returned to Northampton and started housekeeping in a rented apartment. From this they moved into one half of a double house on Massasoit Street, which has been their home ever since. It is a modest but comfortable residence, on a pleasant shaded street in one of the most beautiful cities in the country. In this house the Coolidges continued to live, because it was comfortable and they were satisfied. There was no pose in their remaining there. They simply liked the house and neighborhood.

Little things sometimes have importance

and interest when they concern the lives of the eminent. Thus many young people may take satisfaction in knowing that after the expense of the wedding had been met the young couple had little money. Vigorous debates have been held relative to the amount of money one should have before undertaking matrimony. No authoritative decision has ever been made; but the case of the Coolidges proves that two young people can start life together with a scanty pocketbook and win both happiness and success. It is not likely that in those days Mrs. Coolidge foresaw for herself her present position in the White House. It is said that after Calvin's election to the vice-presidency she was visiting the White House for the first time in many years. A woman in the party asked her if she had ever been there before. Mrs. Coolidge said she had; she explained that when she was a school-teacher she had been there on a sight-seeing trip with other teachers.

"Well," said the other woman, "you certainly have stepped some since then."

That Mrs. Coolidge had faith in the abilities of her husband everyone knows. That she believed a brilliant future to be ahead of him is probable. It is highly improbable, however, that her dreams soared so high as to place him in the highest office of the land. Her own story is not to be told here. Yet no story of Calvin Coolidge is complete or accurate without emphasizing the exceptional qualities of his wife. That she has at all times strengthened him by her faith, and at all times aided him by her gracious personality and social tact, is true.

The Coolidges during all their years of residence in Northampton were attendants at the Congregational Church. Mrs. Coolidge when a young girl joined this church at her home in Vermont, and after her marriage she transferred her membership to the Edwards Congregational Church at Northampton. Edward T. Clark, who has served as private secretary to Mr. Coolidge during his vice-presidency, and who remains a member of the secretarial staff at the White House, is a son of a former pastor of that church. During the Coolidges' residence in Washington they have attended regularly the First Congregational Church, of which the pastor is the Reverend Jason N. Pierce.

Some light is shed on the early Northampton days by Judge Henry P. Field, in whose office Calvin Coolidge studied law. "The thing that impressed itself on my mind," he says, "was the fact that Coolidge believed in the gospel of hard work. He was a plodder, attending strictly to his law studies. He was not one of those chaps who made baseball, football, tennis, and other sports the main thing, and studying law a side issue. He was on the job every day and all day."

Judge Field was a pew-holder in the Edwards Church, and in the first weeks of Coolidge's presence in his office he invited him to occupy part of that pew whenever he wished. Judge Field recalls that he did so with reasonable frequency.

John C. Hammond, senior member of the firm Hammond and Field, says the youth always impressed him as a devout man, who had infinite trust in Divine guidance. It is Mr. Hammond's testimony that the Coolidge youth had a fine respect and reverence for sacred things.

One of the leaders in the Edwards Church of Northampton is Clifford H. Lyman. He recalls the fact that the two Coolidge boys joined the Edwards Church in 1920, while their father was Governor of Massachusetts, and that Governor Coolidge was present on this occasion. "In the early days," said Mr. Lyman, "Mr. Coolidge was active in the Edwards Church Men's Club. He attended the meetings with a good deal of regularity, and I recall that he obtained for us, as speakers, Channing Cox (now Governor of Massachusetts), Lieutenant-Governor Louis A. Frothingham, John N. Cole, a leader in Massachusetts public life, and others."

In conclusion of the mention of Mr. Coolidge's relation to religion, the following quotation from his own writings may here be set down: "It was because religion gave the people a new importance and a new glory that they

demanded a new freedom and a new government. We cannot in our generation reject the
cause and retain the result. If the institutions
they adopted are to survive, if the government
which they founded is to endure, it will be
because the people continue to have similar
religious beliefs. It is idle to discuss freedom
and equality on any other basis. It is useless
to expect substantial reforms from any other
motive. They cannot be administered from
without. They must come from within."

There are many recollections of the Northampton days of Coolidge offered by those who
knew and worked with him then. All picture
a serious-minded young man, a plodder or
digger, distinguished less for brilliancy than
for thoroughness. If one item in his character
stands forth above all others, it is this: he
liked to work. That he was self-contained and
somewhat aloof even in those days is attested
by the reminiscences of his associates. His good
friend, Judge Field, has been quoted referring
to Calvin as "a most inscrutable little devil."

One more reference to the Northampton law period of Coolidge may properly find place here, although it reaches forward to the time of his election to the lieutenant-governorship. It was then necessary for him to take in a partner who should have charge of the office. He selected Ralph W. Hemenway. Thus in the course of time Mr. Hemenway found himself a law partner of a Governor of Massachusetts. A statement lately made by Mr. Hemenway sharply illustrates a vitally important quality in Governor Coolidge: —

"I had never seen Calvin Coolidge until he sent for me and made me the proposition to take up the work of his office as his partner. I have been his partner now for five years. He could, no doubt, have made me rich by reason of his influence and his position, but I can truthfully say that in those five years Mr. Coolidge has not turned me over a dollar's worth of business through political influence or pull. He is not that kind of man. It is not his idea of the proprieties of a public official."

Mr. Coolidge has been charged with ingratitude. If it is a sign of ingratitude for a public
official to refuse to use his office to pay private
debts or to gratify personal friendships, then he
stands convicted. Many men in office do reward
friends, and many do punish enemies, through
the authority of the position to which they
have been elected by the people; and many do
so without consciousness of any impropriety.
Men in posts of political power are in constant
danger of incurring embarrassing obligations.
To do so, and to favor those who have conferred favors, is not necessarily dishonest. Yet,
the inexorable attitude which insists upon a
complete severance between public acts and personal considerations stands unchallengeable.
The statement by Mr. Hemenway is worth
studying.

The next milestone in Coolidge's career
marks his departure from Northampton to enter the Massachusetts House of Representatives
in 1907. His plurality in this first election to
State office was exactly sixty-three votes. Soon

after his election he went to Boston, and, like
other new members, called upon the Speaker of
the House, John N. Cole. He brought a letter
from Richard W. Irwin, of Northampton, a
former State Senator. This letter, addressed to
Speaker Cole, read as follows : —

DEAR JOHN, —

This will introduce the new member-elect from my
town, Calvin Coolidge. Like the singed cat, he is better
than he looks. He wishes to talk with you about committees. Anything you can do for him will be appreci-
ated by

Sincerely yours,
DICK.

IV

IN THE STATE SERVICE

CALVIN COOLIDGE's election to the Legislature marked his transition from the small city to the service of the Commonwealth. He came to Boston by no means a distinguished man beyond the limits of his home town. He was not celebrated. Few took any notice of his arrival, and it is not of record that any prophecies were made for his future. He was simply one of a large number of young men chosen by their neighbors to represent them in the Massachusetts House of Representatives. This is an old and distinguished body of legislators through which have passed, since the beginning of organized government in this country, a long procession of men. From them have been recruited many of those who later became leaders in State and national politics, but the great majority of them serve their districts for a time, either well or ill, go back to their home towns, and are politically forgotten. The lower branch of a State Legislature is not primarily made up of men who have chosen public life for their career. It is composed chiefly of men who have achieved some prominence among their neighbors, and who, their friends believe, can be of service in State legislation. Their participation in public affairs is usually temporary. Therefore there was nothing in the election of Coolidge to the legislature which drew to him any particular attention from political leaders.

Nor was there anything in the behavior or personality of Coolidge upon his arrival in Boston which attracted attention. He appeared to be a modest and somewhat colorless young man. When he presented to Speaker Cole the letter from Richard Irwin, Mr. Cole gave him a friendly but more or less perfunctory greeting, and expressed the amiable desire to do anything he could "for a friend of Dick Irwin." He asked Coolidge if he were a lawyer. Coolidge said he was. "I see," said the Speaker; "I suppose you would like to go on the Judiciary Committee. It is n't customary to put a first-year member on Judiciary. I 'll see what I can do." He was not given a place on this committee. The Speaker assigned him a place on Mercantile Affairs and also on Constitutional Amendments. The former was at that time a quite important committee. Then Mr. Cole appears promptly to have forgotten Mr. Coolidge. Whether or not the new member was a "man of destiny," he obviously made no impression whatever upon the Speaker. Some time later Mr. Coolidge came into Speaker Cole's room, and although the messenger had brought in the name, "Coolidge," it meant little or nothing to him. It was late in April, but in the time which had elapsed since the opening of the session, the busy Speaker of the House had taken little notice of the new member from Northampton.

"I hear you are going to speak in my town next week," said Coolidge. Mr. Cole admitted

that he was. "I'd like to have you spend
the night at my house," said Coolidge. "Glad
to," said the Speaker. With no further conversation, Coolidge departed. Mr. Cole went
to Northampton to speak and was the guest of
Mr. Coolidge in the house at Northampton.
Probably this was the first real notice that John
Cole took of Calvin Coolidge. Their acquaintance ripened into a friendship which lasted
until the death of Mr. Cole in 1922. When Calvin Coolidge as Governor reorganized the State
Departments in 1919, he appointed Mr. Cole
head of the Public Works Department. He was
the holder of that office when he died, and one
of the most efficient public servants in the history of the state.

There is little to be written of Mr. Coolidge's
service during his first year in the lower branch
of the Legislature, except to say that he was a
faithful and conscientious legislator, constant
in attendance at House sessions and committee
meetings. He was in his seat at the beginning
of the day, and remained on duty. He was

quiet of manner, busy — and silent. During the first session he made but one speech, and that was upon some slight matter, of interest chiefly to his district.

We may assume that this first year in the House was a continuance of the education of Mr. Coolidge. His abstention from oratory does not indicate that his year's service was without value to the State or his district. On the contrary, the fidelity of his attention to legislative and committee duties indicates that he was giving serious thought to the matters under discussion. He was the reverse of sensational. The significance of this initiatory period, however, has to do less with what he gave the State than with what he learned, in order — or at least with the result — that he might be better equipped for further service. If there was anything in this first year calculated to increase his own political strength and thus assure his reëlection, it consisted solely in the record of close attention, voting on all roll-calls, and giving to his constituents the correct impression that he was attending to business. That he was studying the nature of legislative processes, that he was familiarizing himself with the manufacture of statutes, we know. That he would under any normal conditions have been reëlected is probable, despite the small margin by which he won his first election to this body. As a candidate for reëlection, he had the considerable asset of being in office, and of having therein established a record which, if not marked by any brilliant achievement, was devoid of offense, and which demonstrated sincerity.

Conditions favored Republican candidacies in the State in the fall, when he came up for reëlection. It was a year of dissension among Massachusetts Democrats. The Democratic Convention split, and two candidates for Governor were placed in the field by that party. This situation made the election of the Republican legislator, Mr. Coolidge, doubly sure in Northampton. He was reëlected by a much increased plurality, and returned to the Legisla-

ture with the benefit of a year's training and
experience behind him. Speaker Cole at once
assigned him to two important committees.
One of these was the Judiciary Committee, to
which he had aspired as a new member, and
for which, as a member of the bar, he obviously
was qualified. The other committee was that
on Banks and Banking. For this also he had a
special equipment, by reason of his connection
as counsel for the Nonotuck Savings Bank in
Northampton.

It is characteristic of Mr. Coolidge's methods
and foresight that he had obtained the maximum benefit from his bank associations in his
home city. That is, having been made counsel
for the bank, he was not satisfied to regard this
simply as a remunerative job; he became recognized almost immediately in Northampton,
and in fact throughout that part of the state,
as an authority on banking laws. While this
increased his usefulness as bank counsel, it did
something far more for him : it established his
reputation in a new and important line.

Whether he foresaw the possible political advantage in this, no one can say. Certainly the accumulation of a reputation for special and authoritative knowledge in important fields creates a reservoir from which a politically ambitious man can always draw. That Mr. Coolidge by this time was politically ambitious, to the extent of having decided upon public life for his career, we may take for granted.

To be sure of facts, and to apply them, is one of the tests of character and one of the means by which men rise. Mr. Coolidge's fortunate equipment for service on the Banks and Banking Committee traces back to an instance which was apparently trivial enough at the time, but which may pertinently be recalled here in connection with this committee appointment. It relates to the early days of Coolidge's presence as a law student in the Northampton office of Hammond and Field. Into the office came one day an elderly man. After waiting in vain for one of the firm to come in, he placed his rather

curious question before young Coolidge. The
question was, whether the selectmen of Had-
ley — of whom the elderly man was one —
had or had not a legal right to remove a dead
body which had been found, before it was
viewed by the medical examiner. Coolidge's
reply consisted of three words : —

"Can remove body."

The caller was rather appalled by the terse-
ness of the young man's speech. It did not
sound lawyer-like to him. Equally, however,
he was impressed by the young man's obvious
assurance. He found the young man's law was
correct. This was the beginning of a friendship
between the two men, and it was shortly after-
ward that Coolidge was brought into the
service of the bank of which the older man was
an official.

In the session of 1908 he did not greatly alter
the course followed by him the year before.
He was always present when a vote was taken,
but he made few speeches. Matters which came
before his committees he investigated very

much as he would have investigated a case brought to his law office. He did not at this time assume any prominent position in party politics, but it did not escape the attention of party leaders that when situations in the House brought party considerations to the fore he could be counted upon to vote with the "regulars." He believed in his party and he stood by it. Again, perhaps unconsciously, he was accumulating a reputation to become serviceable to him later as a leader in his party.

Coolidge's work on the Judiciary and Banking committees brought him in contact with some important legislation. The Banking Committee had before it the task of revising all the banking laws of the Commonwealth. Coolidge's experience as counsel and Vice-President of the Nonotuck Savings Bank was invaluable to him at this time. It was as a member of the Judiciary Committee, however, that he came into more particular prominence. As a member of that committee, he drafted and had charge of an anti-monopoly bill, for which he spoke effectively on the floor of the House. This was probably the first notably active part taken by him which attracted general attention. The bill became law.

As a member of this committee also, he re-drafted an anti-discrimination bill which, on his motion, was substituted by vote of the House for the adverse report of the committee.

By this time he was emerging somewhat from his silence. He was beginning to be heard on the floor of the House. One of the notable speeches in the legislature of 1908 was made by him in favor of a bill reported by the recess Committee on Labor, modifying the law by which injunctions are issued. This bill was much discussed at the time, and Coolidge's speech was one of the most effective factors in the situation. The bill was carried in the House by a large majority.

It will not pass unnoticed that at this stage of his career Mr. Coolidge was actively inter-ested in some very "liberal" legislation. The anti-monopoly bill certainly represented the antithesis of standpattism; so also, the anti-discrimination bill; and so particularly the anti-injunction bill, which he effectively championed on the floor of the House. We may properly repeat here a line of comment from the Northampton *Daily Herald* of April 24, 1908, which said: "Mr. Coolidge is entitled to the thanks of the wage laborers of his district for his manly defense of their interests."

During his first year in the Legislature he went on record in favor of the direct election of the United States Senators. At about the same time he voted in favor of woman suffrage. He championed in that long-distant day a bill designed to prevent cheating in the sale of small lots of coal. He was an earnest advocate of a bill providing for one day's rest in seven. He worked hard and successfully to improve the working-conditions of women and children. He was active in the movement to place surgical equipments in all factories. A bill to pension widows and children of deceased firemen had his support. He favored pensions for public-school teachers; he worked to increase the number of playgrounds for children; he advocated special low fares for workingmen and half fare for schoolchildren.

Was Calvin Coolidge a radical in 1907 and 1908? Has he changed his views regarding liberal legislation in the last fifteen years, or has he not? Certainly his political career since his accession to the governorship of Massachusetts has been generally regarded as marked by conservatism. It probably would be unfair to call him a standpatter, but the label, "conservative," appears warranted by the facts. Discussion of the change of attitude may better be left until we have to consider his service as President of the State Senate in the years 1914 and 1915. Here it may be said that such change of attitude probably indicates — not a change of heart regarding progress and liberalism so much as a realization of the necessity for tempering legislation with a knowledge of the capacity to administer laws under the government. From his own writings of a later date we may take the key which explains his larger measure of conservatism to-day than in 1908.

Before dealing with this point, we have now to consider what may be called an interlude in his State service, comprising the two years, 1910 and 1911, during which he was Mayor of Northampton. From the close of the legislative session in 1908 until he became Mayor in Northampton in 1910 he practised his profession in Northampton and was not an active figure in politics.

His home city had been favorably impressed by his two years in the House of Representatives. Probably the Northampton folks had always understood him. He is of a type more familiar to those of that part of the state than to the residents of the larger cities. No one from western Massachusetts could have made the mistake said to have been made by Martin Lomasney, a leader among Boston Democrats, who is quoted as saying of Coolidge when he first came to Boston to take his seat in the Legislature: "This fellow is either a schoolteacher or an undertaker from the country, I don't know which." The period of political inactivity in Northampton, following his retirement from the House, apparently did nothing to lessen the regard in which he was held by members of his party in that city. In 1909 he was unanimously nominated by the Northampton Republicans as their candidate for Mayor. Campaign "literature" of the period proudly asserts that "the protection of his clients' interests is the business to which Mr. Coolidge's life is devoted. In it he has acquired skill and experience. That skill and experience are now placed at the service of the city in all matters which may concern it." Again: "Well known as a citizen of more than usual business experience, his advice is continually sought by the business and banking interests of the city. Is not this the kind of training, experience, and equipment which the city needs in its Mayor?"

Apparently the voters of Northampton believed the correct answer to be "Yes," for they elected him Mayor and he took office in 1910.

His election followed a hard-fought campaign, however, and his plurality was only 187 votes. At the end of a year he was renominated and reëlected. His plurality this time was 256. On the day following his first election he met on the street a Democratic acquaintance who stopped to congratulate him.

"Congratulations, Cal," he said. "I see you 're elected Mayor — but I did n't vote for you."

"Well," said Calvin, "somebody did."

The service of Mayor Coolidge was satisfactory to his fellow townsmen. That is shown plainly enough by the fact of his election for a second term. What stands particularly to his credit in these two years is the fact that, although he obtained for members of the fire and police departments increases in pay, and also raised the pay of the schoolteachers, his administration reduced the city debt $90,000 and lowered the taxes. These are the only outstanding facts of those two years which command attention now. They showed a capacity for economy which did not obstruct improvements. That his record as Mayor increased his political standing is plainly shown by the fact that in 1912 he was elected to the State Senate from the Berkshire-Hampshire-Hampden district.

This was the time of the Progressive movement and the Bull Moose dissension within the Republican party. As might have been expected from his well-understood party sentiments, Mr. Coolidge did not join that movement. He remained with the older and more conservative part of the Republican party; but he took no part in the quarrel. There was no special reason why he should. He attended strictly to his own affairs and remained a "regular" Republican.

Coolidge entered the State Senate a better-trained man than when he was in the lower branch. The four years spent in practising law and in the office of Mayor had given him valuable experience. While the problems of Northampton were not those of the State, they were not dissimilar in significance, and by his time spent in the office of Mayor he had presumably strengthened his belief that there must be an intimate sympathy and understanding between legislative processes, executive administration, and business. The quality of his administration as Mayor which more than any other stands out as prophetic, was the quality of understanding the need for economy in public expenditures, coupled with progressive improvement in public service. That this need was much on his mind we gather from his subsequent activity of four years in the State Senate.

He was made Chairman of the Senate Committee on Agriculture, and at once became prominent in relation to problems of the milk business in the State. These problems were then undergoing a vigorous and somewhat heated discussion. The subject appealed to Coolidge, doubtless in some part because he was born and raised on a farm. A variety of bills was up for action and the situation was one of confusion, assertion, and counter-assertion. As chairman of the committee he proposed appointment of an expert commission to investigate and clarify the situation. His purpose appears to have been to displace the hysteria and confusion that existed by an orderly presentation of the problem through the commission report, hoping thus to work out something that would be just to all concerned. That is the interpretation placed upon his course by those who followed that notable contest. His resolution for a commission failed. He thereupon vigorously opposed every one of the proposed bills. They were all defeated. Their defeat appears to have satisfied the farmers, who are alleged to have declared most of them impractical measures.

Early in his Senate career he showed a sympathetic interest in the Massachusetts Agricultural College, which is located at Amherst. It was due to his efforts that that institution received an appropriation exceeding by $75,000 any preceding appropriation given it.

Prominence also came to him during that first year in quite another field. The industrial city of Lawrence suffered a labor upheaval. A strike of serious dimensions occurred among the mill workers. The situation became so aggravated that a committee of the Legislature was appointed to investigate it. Coolidge was made chairman of that committee. A settlement of the strike was soon reached, this adjustment including an increase of wages to the operators. Chairman Coolidge was publicly thanked for his part in restoring peace.

This incident of the Lawrence strike is of importance to any biographer of Coolidge. His appointment as chairman of the investigating committee gave the first considerable opportunity to the public to take note of certain qualities he possessed. Friends of Coolidge have often said that there is in him much of the judicial temperament. In the negotiations for settlement of the Lawrence matter this quality was called upon. To enter on such a rôle in the midst of a heated labor-controversy, to effect a settlement which shall give a reasonable degree of satisfaction to all sides, and to emerge from the negotiations with the good will of the public, is not easy. If this experience informed the public concerning Coolidge, it presumably also enlightened Coolidge regarding the serious possibilities ahead in the industrial world of his State. In the years since then he has, to a considerable degree, held the respect and the political support of men active in labor circles, while at the same time he has been liked by representatives of capital.

Some years later a trainman employed by a New England railroad, in explaining why he admired Coolidge, when Governor, said: "It has been my duty to go to the Legislature on matters connected with the Brotherhood now for some five years, and during that time there has been no man on Beacon Hill so fair as Coolidge."

At about the same time the president of one of the New England roads said: "If I should have a dispute with my men and the men were willing to leave the question to Coolidge as sole arbiter, I would be willing that they should argue their case and I would be quite content to leave my case without argument."

During his second year in the Senate he was Chairman of the Committee on Railroads. It is significant that every single report of the committee that year was sustained by the Senate. His friends say this was due to the fact that he was thorough in the committee work, and that each matter was carefully gone over before the reports were put in form.

At the beginning of his third year of Senate service, 1914, he was chosen President. His address on that occasion has been called one of the most notable political utterances on record. It has been much quoted, and many are familiar in particular with that passage which has been referred to as the "Coolidge creed." Although so familiar, it may properly be set down again here because, more than any utterance by him up to that time, it established in the public mind the thought that he might eventually become a leader in his party and the State. The paragraph is as follows: —

"Do the day's work. If it be to protect the rights of the weak, whoever objects, do it. If it be to help a powerful corporation better to serve the people, whatever the opposition, do that. Expect to be called a standpatter, but don't be a standpatter. Expect to be called a demagogue, but don't be a demagogue. Don't hesitate to be as revolutionary as science. Don't hesitate to be as reactionary as the multiplication table. Don't expect to build up the weak by pulling down the strong. Don't hurry to legislate. Give administration a chance to catch up with legislation."

In the two concluding sentences of that paragraph may be found the explanation of Coolidge's increasing conservatism. Some years later he told a friend that when he first entered the Legislature he was considered a radical, particularly along lines of legislation favoring social betterment. His experience of two years in the House and a year or two in the Senate impressed upon him the belief, not that his ideas in favor of humanitarian purposes were wrong, but that many States, including Massachusetts, were going too fast. Legislation was moving faster than the power to administer. He began to distrust the wisdom of undertaking by legislative process alone to effect ends which required for their consummation a carefully constructed and effectively directed scheme of administration. When he told the Senate not to hurry in legislation, but to give administration a chance to catch up, he was stating publicly for the first time the fruit of that thought.

It is important to remember this when we undertake to classify him in relation to his subsequent attitude in matters of legislation and administration. That effective government requires a delicate and accurate adjustment of machinery, and that the making of laws is only a single portion of that machinery, is an obvious fact familiar to all students of history. The time of his election to the Senate presidency is marked for Coolidge by his newly stirred attention to the importance of the administrative side of government. A fact to be emphasized —

in view of future events then unforeseen — is that, while still a legislator, he was beginning to think also from the viewpoint of an executive.

In this same address to the Senate are many phrases which attracted attention then and which now are worth re-quoting because the man who made them is President of the nation. For example : —

"Men do not make laws. They do but discover them."

"Courts are established, not to determine the popularity of a cause, but to adjudicate and enforce rights."

"The people cannot look to legislation generally for success. Industry, thrift, character, are not conferred by Act or Resolve. Government cannot relieve from toil; it can provide no substitute for the rewards of service. . . . Self-government means self-support."

"Statutes must appeal to more than material welfare. Wages won't satisfy, be they never so large; nor houses; nor lands; nor coupons,

though they fall thick as the leaves of autumn.
Man has a spiritual nature. Touch it, and it
must respond as the magnet responds to the
pole. To that, not to selfishness, let the laws
of the Commonwealth appeal.''

Mr. Coolidge presided over the Senate with
discretion and impartiality. Frequently he left
the chair and spoke from the floor in support of
or in opposition to bills under consideration.
The next year he was reëlected to preside.
Remembering the notable address of the preceding January, there was much curiosity as
to what he would say this time. His speech
was as follows : —

''Honorable Senators, my sincerest thanks I
offer you. Conserve the firm foundations of our
institutions. Do your work with the spirit of
a soldier in the public service. Be loyal to the
Commonwealth and to yourselves. And be
brief; above all things, be brief.''

That was all. In quite another way this
speech made as much of a sensation as the other.

There were occasions of storm in the Senate,

and these Mr. Coolidge handled with tact. In one such case an excited Senator told a fellow member that he might "go to hell." The aggrieved one rushed up the aisle waving his hand and shouted at Mr. Coolidge, who was presiding, "Did you hear what he said?"

"Yes," said Coolidge, "I heard what he said. But I've looked up the law and you don't have to do it."

That ended the incident. There was no fight.

The period of his presidency of the Senate was marked by an event destined to have great consequences. The friendship between Calvin Coolidge and Frank W. Stearns was formed at this time. Mr. Stearns called on Mr. Coolidge in behalf of a bill affecting Amherst College, of which Mr. Stearns was a trustee. He had the unexpected experience of meeting a refusal. Mr. Coolidge did not take the same view of the bill as did Mr. Stearns. The independence of this young man and the quietness of his manner impressed the older. That was the real beginning of their acquaintance, which ultimately developed into a friendship perhaps unique in the history of politics. One day, soon after Coolidge succeeded to the presidency of the nation, Mr. Stearns summed up his relations with Coolidge, in conversation with a friend : "In a social way I feel like a father to Calvin Coolidge. In a political way I feel like a son to him." Mr. Stearns has never desired or sought to exert any political influence over Mr. Coolidge, or to recommend or oppose any appointment or legislation. He picked out Coolidge as a man who could and should go far politically. He said he would some day see him President of the United States. He did not utter it so much as a prophecy, as an emphatic way of expressing his admiration. Yet as a prophecy it might well stand.

It was Mr. Stearns who guided Coolidge toward the lieutenant-governorship, to which he was elected in 1916.

V

AS AN EXECUTIVE

ANOTHER milestone here marks the turning of Calvin Coolidge toward the path that leads upward through executive office toward the presidency. Whether he would have started upon this path without the impetus given him by Mr. Stearns's encouragement, no one can say; it is likely that he would have done so in any event. It undoubtedly would have been slower progress but for the man who was to become his good friend. The bill concerning which Mr. Stearns had approached Coolidge, a bill authorizing Amherst College to connect with the town sewerage system, was passed by the Legislature of the next year. Senator Coolidge's objection to it had been that it was offered too late in the session.

Meantime the attention of Mr. Stearns had been attracted and held, and the possibility of

advancing Coolidge to the lieutenant-governorship had taken a strong hold on Mr. Stearns's
imagination. Their acquaintance was still new
when Mr. Stearns suggested to him that he
should be a candidate. Coolidge would give
no decided answer. Not until the Senate had
adjourned did he make any definite statement.
He then announced his candidacy in just fifty
words. When Mr. Stearns asked him why he
had not earlier agreed to be a candidate, he said
he had not thought it right for him to make
any announcement while the Senate was in
session. "I could not have acted like myself if
I had announced my candidacy during the session. No matter what I did or said, it would
have been misconstrued, and there would have
been thirty-nine candidates to succeed me as
President of the Senate. It would have inter-
fered with the public business of the Senate."
The propriety of his attitude is obvious; less
obvious but equally worth note is the fact that
it was good politics.

That Mr. Stearns was the first man to detect

presidential qualities in Coolidge is a fact un-
disputed. It is not of record that he expressed
any such thought at the time when he was
urging him to be a candidate for Lieutenant-
Governor. What he certainly did believe he
saw in Coolidge at that time was an equipment
well fitted for political advancement. He had
faith that in the office of Lieutenant-Governor
he would demonstrate qualities which would
lead him higher. It was after his becoming
Lieutenant-Governor, in 1916, that he first made
public suggestion of Coolidge as timber for
nomination as the Republican candidate for
President.

Election to the lieutenant-governorship is,
under Massachusetts political custom, directly
preliminary to a nomination for Governor.
Therefore in urging his friend to be candidate
for the minor office, Mr. Stearns's objective
was the governorship. This was well understood. A dinner was given, attended chiefly by
a number of Amherst graduates. At this dinner
Coolidge was toasted (in cold water) as "the

future Governor of Massachusetts." Testimony
is to the effect that at this dinner Coolidge
maintained his discreet and customary silence.

In the summer of 1915, Grafton D. Cushing,
then Lieutenant-Governor, became a candidate
for the Republican nomination for Governor
against Samuel W. McCall. It was late in June,
and some time after the Cushing statement, that
Coolidge announced his candidacy for nomination to second place on the ticket. His statement was characteristic : —

"I am a candidate for Lieutenant-Governor.
This announcement is made for the purpose of
informing my fellow citizens of my plans. I
shall discuss my reasons for being a candidate
and place before the voters an expression of my
views upon those issues which confront the
people of Massachusetts."

Possibly the situation at that time was a
manifestation of "Coolidge luck." Certainly
Cushing's unfortunate decision to oppose
McCall made a very wide opening into which
Coolidge sagaciously stepped with this an-

nouncement of his candidacy for second place.
In the somewhat confused political situation
then existing, Mr. Coolidge's judgment was
accurate and forevisioned. A misjudgment by
him at that time, a yielding to the temptation
to enter what appeared about to be a free-for-all
race for the governorship, might have eliminated him permanently, or at least have long
delayed his political advancement.

In his statement he said that he should discuss his reasons for being a candidate. He did
so in a few simple speeches. Two other candidates for the lieutenant-governorship were
under consideration by his party. One of
them, Colonel Goetting of Springfield, with-
drew almost immediately after the Coolidge
announcement. There remained Guy A. Ham,
of Boston, to compete with Coolidge for the
nomination. Many thought it an unequal contest with the odds in favor of Mr. Ham. He
had been earlier in the field and advanced his
candidacy by brilliant speeches; he held high
reputation as one of the most effective stump

speakers among the younger Republicans. His
supporters were confident that he would dis-
pose of Coolidge in short order. His contri-
bution to the primary campaign exceeded that
of Coolidge notably in the number of speeches.
He had what is vaguely called "magnetism,"
he had the ability to present his case elo-
quently, and there was no point in his career
which could be interpreted as indicating weakness before the voters. Nevertheless, when the
ballots were counted, the result stood: Coolidge, 74,592; Ham, 50,401. Coolidge had carried every county except Norfolk and Suffolk.
In these two counties the total majority against
him was less than one thousand. McCall's
nomination was a foregone conclusion. Mc-
Call and Coolidge thus became the ticket, and
they toured the State together. The Democratic
candidate was David I. Walsh, a popular man.
The Democratic candidate for Lieutenant-Governor was Edward Barry. McCall's plurality
in the election was 6000; Coolidge's plurality
was 46,000. Some allowance must be made for

the standing of David Walsh, who was a better known man than Barry. Nevertheless, the fact that Coolidge ran so far ahead of the veteran statesman, McCall, impressed political leaders in both parties. This election was the first test of Coolidge's strength throughout the state.

The office of Lieutenant-Governor of Massachusetts is not a sinecure. He not only acts for the Governor in his absence, but he has specific duties of his own. He presides over the Executive Council. The Council is an elected body of eight members who have well-defined work to do. They supervise State commissions and institutions—including prisons and hospitals—and they scrutinize public expenditures. Politically they have an even more important function in that their advice and consent are necessary to validate appointments made by the Governor. To this office Coolidge brought the same inclination to take his job seriously that he had demonstrated elsewhere. His interest in the State institutions was not merely perfunctory. He personally visited them.

One instance will serve to illustrate his method as Lieutenant-Governor. A young man had been appointed as a pilot in Plymouth Harbor. There was some doubt among shipping men of the wisdom of that appointment. The appointee was a young man of good character, but his experience with the channel had been confined to small vessels, such as fishing boats. He had had no experience whatever with large steamers. Therefore, establishments which received cargoes by such steamers in Plymouth were apprehensive. One day the head of a large firm interested in this situation appeared before the Executive Council in relation to this appointment. He remained in the Council chamber for some time. When he came out, a man who was waiting for an opportunity to see the Lieutenant-Governor asked him: "Is Coolidge in there?"

The man's reply was: "There was a man in there that looked something like his picture, who said nothing, and apparently was not paying much attention."

The same two men met a fortnight later, and the shipping man said : "That man Coolidge is a star. I thought he was paying no attention. I was wrong. I find that he wrote at once to Plymouth to learn all the facts, he went personally to the wharves, talked with the pilots of Boston Harbor, learned about the duties of a pilot, and he now has worked out a plan for correcting the troubles at Plymouth."

This was the period of his career which first impressed upon the public throughout the State his singular gift for silence. Those who had followed public affairs in the Legislature were familiar with his curious ways. But there is a large portion of the public which pays no attention to legislative matters, and to whom members of the Great and General Court are unknown. The Governor and Lieutenant-Governor, however, are marked figures in the public eye. Everyone in or out of politics knows who they are and has some degree of interest in their personalities. Coolidge had not long been Lieutenant-Governor before he was celebrated as an "eloquent listener." The State was beginning to take stock of him.

During the campaign Coolidge's speeches had been confined almost exclusively to argument in behalf of the election of McCall to the governorship. He said little of his own candidacy. This was commented on by the press at the time. The same loyalty to his chief was a characteristic of his service during three years as Lieutenant-Governor. He was often called upon, as the Lieutenant-Governor is bound to be, to represent the Commonwealth at public affairs, attendance at which was inconvenient for the Governor. These official speeches are usually of a perfunctory nature and are marked chiefly by an expression of the good will of the State. Into them Lieutenant-Governor Coolidge put a good deal of his political philosophy. This consisted of an expression of faith in American character, an assertion of the need for strength and conscience in political affairs, and respect for politics as the art of government. There was in these speeches no assertion of his personal ambitions. They were graceful and adequate utterances of a dignified State official. It is probable that they served to strengthen public confidence in the administration of which Governor McCall was the chief.

It is pertinent to emphasize the quality of Coolidge's loyalty to his chief and his party at this period of his career. It is necessary, if we are to understand this man and gauge his administration at Washington correctly, to recognize the vital fact that he is constitutionally faithful to that which he believes to be good. He is unwavering in his devotion to the Republican party because he is essentially a party man; he is similarly loyal to his immediate political superior because that is the natural bent of his mind. As Lieutenant-Governor he was at all times conscious of his obligation to the Governor. The same quality was shown by him as Vice-President of the United States.

He served as Lieutenant-Governor for three

years, Massachusetts at that time holding annual elections. Each year his plurality increased, and in 1917 it was 101,731. It was a logical result that, on the retirement of Governor McCall, Coolidge was the unopposed candidate of his party for Governor. During his years as Lieutenant-Governor he had prepared the public's mind for the ideas he would presumably represent as Governor. In his campaign speeches, while he urged the voters to support McCall, he inserted a large measure of his own philosophy of government, coupled with partisan appeal. As this was the period in which he was first presenting his personality before the State as an aspirant for executive office, it is important to recognize the fact that he yoked so closely his theories of government and his intensely practical belief in his own political party. An extract from one of his campaign speeches, when he was a candidate for Lieutenant-Governor, will serve to illustrate with precision this association of ideas and purposes in his mind. At that time the matter of government supervision of industries was under discussion by many speakers and writers. The flavor of Coolidge's speeches indicated no hostility to such supervision, wisely administered and directed to the purpose of construction and strength. Bear in mind that he was speaking as a Republican and with rigorous party convictions. He was sharply critical of the opposition party. This was obvious party politics; that it represented a basic belief in the superiority of his own party is not doubted. The extract from one of his speeches which shows his position is as follows : —

"Ruthless and unskilled interference is breaking down our industries. The slim margin of profit is vanishing under the expense of unbusinesslike restrictions. You need the Republican standard in the appointing power; you need it to control and supervise commissions. Unless this is speedily restored, danger and destruction wait on Massachusetts as an industrial State. Give us a Republican administration that will make appointments on merit, not political expediency. Let us return to Republican ideals of supervision under the law; we do not need more legislation. Repeal even is unnecessary. What Massachusetts needs — what the nation needs — is a wise administration of the law. Look not to the Legislature for relief; look to the Executive.''

In these speeches he was, of course, intent upon a candidate for an executive office; while he was advancing his own cause, he was even more notably pleading for the candidate for Governor. Obviously, the objectives he presents in the quotation above were attainable not through the Lieutenant-Governor, but through the Chief Executive of the Commonwealth. Yet it will not escape attention that he was presenting to the voters a distinctly individual attitude toward public affairs, and that he was implanting in their minds a distinct image of himself. We do not need to assume that in doing so he was deliberately creating for himself an asset for future availability; in fairness we must conclude rather that he saw in his candidacy for state office an immediate opportunity to preach a gospel of government which was no new thing to him, but which he had not until then been able to present to so wide an audience.

Setting aside as of passing importance the purely partisan appeal in the foregoing quotation, we find the real meat of the matter in the concluding sentences: "What Massachusetts needs — what the nation needs — is a wise administration of the law. Look not to the Legislature for relief; look to the Executive." It will have been kept in mind that this is precisely the same doctrine he had preached as President of the Senate, when he told the State Senators not to be in any hurry to legislate, but to give administration a chance to catch up with legislation. It will be recalled, also, that the process by which he had modified his early haste in social legislation, a process which brought him into the classification of the conservatives, was simply a process forced by his own personal conviction that an oversupply of legislation

contemporary with an inadequacy of administration would produce in the body politic
derangements as serious as would follow a
man's consumption of food beyond his powers
of digestion. The popular tendency in seeking relief from unsatisfactory conditions is
always in the direction of legislative activity.
Petitions in behalf of popular causes usually
make their appeal directly to lawmaking bodies
in city, state, or nation. Organized public
efforts to obtain better conditions through the
medium of administrative processes are rare.
The legislator always seems nearer to the
individual than does the executive. The link
joining the legislature to the public is more
apparent than that which connects with the
executive. Thus there are two forces almost
constantly operating to accelerate legislation.
One is the direct pressure of public appeal
abetted by agitations variously conceived;
the other is the political sensitiveness of holders
of legislative office and their spontaneous reaction to any suggested course likely to increase

their popularity in their districts. Many students of government affairs have recognized the fact that this combination of causes of lawmaking restlessness suggests a danger, as well as an opportunity, under democratic government. How to apply the brakes so as to prevent legislative runaways, without at the same time retarding proper progress, is one of the problems of statesmanship.

In analyzing the character and career of Coolidge it is essential to see that this problem was much upon his mind almost from the moment when he attained a position of responsibility in state affairs. Sharing at first the common lust for laws, he soon realized the existence of this problem, and in his utterances as President of the State Senate the fruit of his reflections began to appear. In his first appeal to the whole electorate of the State he seized the opportunity to impress on the public these same convictions. In doing so he undoubtedly served the candidate for Governor, because he was focusing attention upon what he believed to be the importance of choosing a man of statesmanlike qualities for that office. Throughout his several campaigns for Lieutenant-Governor, while he appealed directly and effectively for the head of the ticket, and for his political party, he was implanting firmly a definite picture of himself.

Coolidge was the unopposed candidate of his party for Governor of Massachusetts in 1918. His opponent at the polls was Richard H. Long, nominated by the Democratic party. Coolidge won with a plurality of 17,035. He carried into office the political philosophy indicated in his official speeches and in his campaigns. This did not, however, prevent him from aiding and approving a considerable list of laws which may fairly be classed as progressive. In the field of labor legislation, for example, he signed bills providing for a forty-eight hour working-week for women and children; a requirement that labor specifications be furnished to textile weavers; a two-platoon system for firemen in

cities and towns which should accept the act;
a bill allowing the representation of employees
on directorates of manufacturing corporations;
requiring posting of decrees of the minimum
wage commission by employers affected; increasing maximum weekly payments from $14
to $16 under the workmen's compensation law;
providing weekly payment of compensation in
cases of partial incapacity.

As Governor he was in some degree instru-
mental in obtaining legislation designed to
meet popular demands at that time, and also
of permanent importance in the state. These
included laws whose purpose was to check
profiteering landlords; authorizing cities and
towns to take property by eminent domain to
provide dwellings in times of emergency (this
being a measure called for by an acute shortage
of housing facilities); giving courts power to
stay eviction proceedings six months under certain circumstances (this being legislation also
demanded by the housing situation); penaliz-
ing landlords who omitted to keep agreements

regarding heat, light, and similar service; establishing the office of fuel administrator, to correct abuses incidental to the fuel situation at that time; providing for reforestation of one hundred thousand acres of waste Massachusetts land; creating a commission to care for the graves of Massachusetts soldiers buried in France; to regulate outdoor advertising; reducing the cost of trial for claims of less than $35; extending authority to town governments; enlarging the power and usefulness of coöperative banks; authorizing the appointment of an unpaid commission to investigate the subject of maternity benefits and to report with recommendations to the General Court.

Governor Coolidge entered upon his duties soon after the conclusion of the World War. Much legislation concerning the service men was presented and enacted in the Legislature during the first year of his governorship. He signed, during that year, bills providing a one-hundred-dollar State bonus for World War veterans; giving preference in public appointment to veterans; creating a commission to find employment for veterans; continuing State aid for dependents for two months after a veteran's death; authorizing cities and towns to spend money to welcome veterans home; creating a new voluntary State Militia, with the Yankee (26th) Division as a nucleus; preserving the standing of service members in the State-employment system, and preserving the civil-service ratings of veterans; continuing the exemption from poll taxes of veterans while in service; authorizing cities and towns to lease quarters for American Legion posts; authorizing the use of State armories for veterans.

Despite the considerable mass of legislation which he either encouraged or approved, Governor Coolidge retained his belief in the need for administration to catch up with legislation. This is shown clearly in his inaugural address at the beginning of his second term, January 9, 1920. Before this event, the dramatic incident of the police strike had intervened. That chapter is of so great importance that it must be left for separate consideration. The passage in his second inaugural address to which reference is here made contains this : —

"In general, it is time to conserve, to retrench rather than to reform, a time to stabilize the administration of the present laws rather than to seek new legislation."

When he made this address he was under consideration as a possible candidate of the Republican party for the presidency of the United States. He attained to a position of peculiar prominence as a result of the police strike. Therefore his reiteration of his familiar emphasis upon the needs of administration was of new and large significance. While the words were addressed first to the Massachusetts legislature and, second, to the people of Massachusetts, it must have been in his mind that they would be read also by a considerable number of persons throughout the country. Probably no one would accuse him of deliberately addressing the nation through the medium of a State inaugural address; yet it must have been a source of satisfaction to him to believe that his favorite convictions regarding legislation and administration would now have a wider audience. Mr. Coolidge had become a national figure. He knew this to be true. However reluctant he may have been to discuss, even with his closest friends, the future which was so vibrant with possibilities, in his own mind he must have foreseen opening before him a vista unlimited. That he shaped his course in any way to further his own chances for political advancement in national politics does not at any point appear. We can find no trace in any of his writings or public speeches, or in any informal reports of his conversation with friends, of any effort by him to advance himself beyond the office which he then occupied.

There remains a matter of large importance which must be discussed as indicating permanent results from his administration as Governor. This has to do with the reorganization of the State departments, following the action of a State Constitutional Convention. The incident is pertinent, not only because of its effect upon the State service organization, but because it is one of the most striking instances available marking the methods of Mr. Coolidge and setting forth the curious ability he appears to have to combine governmental processes with adroit political proceedings. The State Constitutional Convention had suggested an amendment under which the Legislature was required to reduce the number of departments of administration, which was 118, to not more than 20; it further required that the Legislature should effect this reduction within not more than three years. Governor Coolidge accomplished this reduction, after the amendment had been accepted, in less than one year. In stating his purpose to carry out immediately the mandate of the amendment, he informed the chief holders of office under the existing departments that he would not approve any activity on their part in opposing such immediate reduction. This was one of the most effective instances of administrative achieve-

ment in the records of State politics. The reorganization having been commanded, it had
devolved upon the Governor to carry out the
command. He did so expeditiously and with a
surprisingly small amount of subsequent criticism. While the credit for the greater economy
of State government contemplated in this reorganization must go to the Constitutional
Convention and to the Legislature which devised the plan, full credit for the precision
with which the plan was put into operation
goes to the Governor.

It is obvious that in any such reorganization,
and reduction in the number of State administrative departments, many men must be removed from office or at least reduced in rank.
It is equally obvious that such reorganization
provides opportunity for new appointees. In
his selections, both for removal and for advancement, Governor Coolidge appears to have
been singularly fortunate in avoiding disastrous political consequences to himself and
in strengthening the personnel of the State's

government organization. Not all his appointments met unanimous approval. Some honest critics believed that in some instances better selections could have been made. There was, however, not the slightest whisper of scandal or petty politics following the announcement of the list.

On the day following the announcement of the appointments a few temperate criticisms were offered in editorial columns; these were overshadowed by one dramatic outburst of protest and criticism from a man prominent in partisan political affairs. This indignant man voiced his anger to such an extent that it may be believed to have silenced or prevented other criticism which otherwise might have been offered on less personal grounds. Personal friends and political associates of this vociferous critic had been eliminated from office by Governor Coolidge's act, and the man himself had been offered an insignificant office, carrying a salary of just one thousand dollars per year. There is no authority for saying that Governor

Coolidge deliberately courted this outburst of excessive and intemperate criticism. If he did, it was a move of the utmost political cleverness. If he did not, it may be set down perhaps as another instance of "Coolidge luck." After this man had uttered his blast, any further criticism of the Governor's action and appointments must have appeared as support for the outraged political victim. It is fair to suppose that the almost unanimous silence, or at least abstention from criticism, was in large measure due to this circumstance.

Certainly in one aspect of the Governor's procedure, political astuteness was shown. It had been generally supposed that these appointments would be made a few at a time. His decision to make them all at once was wise. Criticism, instead of being invited by each instance of a change in personnel, was concentrated into a single opportunity. The political advantage in this is clear. Also it will not escape attention that he kept his own counsel preceding the announcement. None knew precisely when he would speak, and none knew whom he would appoint. The list was in many respects a complete surprise to those who supposed themselves politically well informed.

Of all the acts of Mr. Coolidge during his two years as Governor, this probably is the most important, except his share in the police strike situation. He himself regards this as his most effective work for efficient government done by him as the Governor of the Commonwealth. To take the entire governing machinery of a State, to remake it from top to bottom, to consolidate many departments, to eliminate many individuals in office and, having strong political connections, to inject new energy into administration, and to do this with the minimum of delay, is an achievement of the first rank. To do so without bringing about his head a storm of attack indicates political sagacity.

Two vetoes stand out particularly to mark his occupancy of the office : one was his veto of a bill whose purpose was to legalize in Massachusetts the sale of beer with an alcoholic content of 2.75 per cent. In this veto he pointed out that the bill "would provide no beer for the people." He said that "no one would dare act under it, or, if anyone should do so, he would certainly be charged with crime." He stated his opposition to "the practice of a legislative deception." It had been prophesied that if he vetoed the bill it would bring upon him political disaster. It did not do so. His other notable veto was of a bill increasing the salaries of members of the legislature. In it he called attention to the fact that service in the Legislature was not compulsory. In this instance, too, it was said that his veto would cost him his popularity with the lawmakers. It did not do so.

Calvin Coolidge was succeeded by Channing Cox as Governor of Massachusetts on January 6, 1921. On January 10, in looking over some papers on his desk, Governor Cox chanced to displace the desk blotter. He saw under it an envelope addressed to him. Wondering what it was, he opened it and found this note : —

My DEAR GOVERNOR COX, —

I want to leave you my best wishes, my assurance of support, and my confidence in your success.

Cordially yours,

CALVIN COOLIDGE.

Governor Coolidge had written this note a few moments before he left the office on January 6. An act of courtesy to his successor was thus his last act in the office of Governor of Massachusetts.

VI

THE POLICE STRIKE AND ITS CONSEQUENCES

ON September 9, 1919, nearly three fourths of the Boston patrolmen left their posts. The exact number was 1117 out of a total of 1544. The immediate result was a condition approximating anarchy in Boston. This incident is commonly referred to as the "police strike." The most momentous political consequence of the affair was the sudden and dramatic rise of Calvin Coolidge to national prominence. It is not within the province of this book to discuss the causes of that action by the police. A controversy continuing to this day has persisted, relative to the respective parts played during those exciting days by Edwin U. Curtis, Police Commissioner of Boston,[1] Andrew J. Peters,

[1] For those unfamiliar with Boston government, it may be explained that the police department of the city is headed by a Commissioner appointed by the Governor. Commissioner Curtis had been appointed by Samuel W. McCall in December 1918.

Mayor of Boston, and Calvin Coolidge, Governor of Massachusetts. Let us address ourselves here to matters beyond dispute.

The specific occasion of the strike, so-called, was an assertion by the patrolmen of an intention to affiliate with the American Federation of Labor. Their claim that they had a right to do so was denied by Commissioner Curtis. Members of the police force persisted, with the immediate result that the Commissioner preferred charges against certain known members of the union and ordered their suspension pending a formal hearing. The charges were sustained. The strike followed. Disorder came upon the city. Store-windows were smashed, goods were stolen, gambling games were openly conducted on Boston Common, and a general condition of lawlessness prevailed on the night of September 9 and during a portion of the following day. Troops were utilized to restore order and under Commissioner Curtis a new police force was recruited and organized. Military forces in the meantime, and for a considerable period, performed police duty. Commissioner Curtis had the unqualified support of the Governor in his refusal to allow the affiliation proposed by the members of the police.

The issue was more than a local one. It involved the whole question of police responsibility in all cities. The point at issue was whether it was allowable and endurable that the members of a police force should owe allegiance to any authority other than that of the constituted head of their department. This issue was acute in many American cities at that time. The crisis occurred in Boston. The handling of that crisis attracted national attention. Governor Coolidge was the spectacular figure, and his course, as indicated by reports of the affair and by his official statements, received national commendation.

Whatever measure of credit should go to Mayor Peters and to Commissioner Curtis, the fact remains beyond controversy that the issue was crystallized for public understanding by the official documents in the case emanating from

the Governor's office. The issue was larger
than one of any personality, for it dealt with
fundamental considerations of government. A
sharp question arose, whether the supreme
authority was the constituted government or
something else. The supremacy of government
was asserted with irresistible force by Governor Coolidge. It was his doing so, and the
manner of his doing so, which impressed the
entire country. The detailed history of the
police strike is long and intricate. There is
nothing intricate or confusing in the statement
of the issue as made by Governor Coolidge.
This was clear, and it was understood. The
act of suppressing disorder and anarchy, the
act of preventing consummation of the plans
of the Boston police to affiliate with the American Federation of Labor, the act of creating a
new police force — all these are of great importance; we are here concerned, however, not
with those acts, but with an inquiry into the
reason why Calvin Coolidge became at one
leap a figure to command national interest.

We find the explanation in two proclamations and a telegram written by him. There are several documents in the case of the police strike which are of historical interest, but these three sum up the entire situation.

There is more involved here than the Boston police strike. There are involved the personality and the convictions of an individual suddenly exhibited before the country. What the people of the United States saw first was the drama of the immediate occasion; second, they saw revealed a conception of government which met their own beliefs and desires. They heard a voice saying precisely what they wanted to hear said. If we are to understand at all the sensational interest suddenly aroused by Coolidge, we have to recognize this fact: no solution of the Boston police strike, no matter how righteous and courageous, could have attracted such attention or could have exalted in public estimation any individual, except for the inclusion in that settlement of a crystallization of national thought concerning vital principles of law, order, and government. The statements of Governor Coolidge revealed qualities which captured the imagination and the approval of the country.

The first of the three revealing documents is a proclamation given September 11, 1919, in which Governor Coolidge said : —

"The entire State Guard of Massachusetts has been called out. Under the Constitution the Governor is the Commander-in-Chief thereof, by an authority of which he could not, if he chose, divest himself. That command I must and will exercise. Under the law I hereby call on all the police of Boston who have loyally and in a never-to-be-forgotten way remained on duty to aid me in the performance of my duty of the restoration and maintenance of order in the City of Boston, and each of such officers is required to act in obedience to such orders as I may hereafter issue or cause to be issued. I call on every citizen to aid me in the maintenance of law and order."

On the same day Governor Coolidge issued

Executive Order No. 1, directing Commissioner Curtis to proceed in the performance of his duties as Police Commissioner under his command.

On September 14, Governor Coolidge addressed to Samuel Gompers, President of the American Federation of Labor, the telegram which aroused national attention and in which occurs the phrase, "there is no right to strike against the public safety by anybody, anywhere, any time." This telegram is one of the most effective official documents on record anywhere. It is here produced in full, because it constitutes that revelation of Coolidge which was the foundation of his status as a national figure. It is as follows : —

"Replying to your telegram, I have already refused to remove the Police Commissioner of Boston. I did not appoint him. He can assume no position which the courts would uphold except what the people have by the authority of their law vested in him. He speaks only with their voice. The right of the police of Boston to affiliate has always been questioned, never granted, is now prohibited. The suggestion of President Wilson to Washington does not apply to Boston. There the police have remained on duty. Here the Policemen's Union left their duty, an action which President Wilson characterized as a crime against civilization. Your assertion that the Commissioner was wrong cannot justify the wrong of leaving the city unguarded. That furnished the opportunity, the criminal element furnished the action. There is no right to strike against the public safety by anybody, anywhere, any time. You ask that the public safety again be placed in the hands of these same policemen while they continue in disobedience to the laws of Massachusetts and in their refusal to obey the orders of the Police Department. Nineteen men have been tried and removed. Others having abandoned their duty, their places have, under the law, been declared vacant on the opinion of the Attorney-General. I can suggest no authority outside the courts to take further action. I wish to join and assist in taking a broad view of every situation. A grave responsibility rests on all of us. You can depend on me to support you in every legal action and sound policy. I am equally determined to defend the sovereignty of Massachusetts and to maintain the authority and jurisdiction over her public officers where it has been placed by the Constitution and laws of her people."

No reply to this telegram was received.

A curious attitude on the part of some of the public now manifested itself. Many men, whose sincerity and good purpose was not open to question, felt that the police strike was broken; not only that there was no need for further action, but that the interests of effective police service would best be served by yielding to what they conceived to be public sentiment and by consenting to a restoration to duty of some, at least, of the policemen who left their posts. How mistaken that attitude was, how disastrous would have been surrender to it, has since become clear to all. It is a fact, however, that at the time strong pressure was brought to bear upon the Governor to compromise the case at this point. He refused to do so.

There is a story to the effect that one man, representing many who had talked the case over, went to see him. He told Governor Coolidge that it was their fear that if he persisted in his unrelenting attitude toward the former policemen it would prevent his reëlection as Governor. The election was but a few weeks ahead. It was assumed by these timid ones that the Governor's attitude would hopelessly alienate organized labor throughout the state, and that every industrial centre would rally to the support of his opponent, Richard H. Long. According to the account of the incident, Governor Coolidge's only reply to that presentation of the case was: —

"It does not matter whether I am elected or not."

Nevertheless, for the ten days following publication of the Coolidge telegram to Gom-

pers, the effort to obtain reinstatement for the
police persisted and assumed dangerous proportions. It was ended by a proclamation which
Governor Coolidge gave, September 24. In this
he restated the issue and compelled the conclusion so clearly that there remained no possibility for further argument. The process of
forming a new police force throughout — except for those men who had remained on duty
and who were, of course, retained in the new
organization — had been menaced by the agitation which Governor Coolidge by this proclamation silenced. It is here reproduced in full,
as the third and final document in the police
strike incident, so far as it concerns the status
of its author : —

"There appears to be a misapprehension as
to the position of the police of Boston. In the
deliberate intention to intimidate and coerce
the government of this Commonwealth a large
body of policemen, urging all others to join
them, deserted their posts of duty, letting in
the enemy. This act of theirs was voluntary,

against the advice of their well-wishers, long discussed and premeditated, and with the purpose of obstructing the power of the government to protect its citizens or even to maintain its own existence. Its success meant anarchy. By this act, through the operation of the law they dispossessed themselves. They went out of office. They stand as though they had never been appointed.

"Other police remained on duty. They are the real heroes of this crisis. The State Guard responded most efficiently. Thousands have volunteered for the Guard and the Militia. Money has been contributed from every walk of life by the hundreds of thousands for the encouragement and relief of these loyal men. These acts have been spontaneous, significant, and decisive. I propose to support all those who are supporting their own government with every power which the people have entrusted to me.

"There is an obligation, inescapable, no less solemn, to resist all those who do not support

the government. The authority of the Commonwealth cannot be intimidated or coerced.
It cannot be compromised. To place the maintenance of the public security in the hands of a
body of men who have attempted to destroy it
would be to flout the sovereignty of the laws
the people have made. It is my duty to resist
any such proposal. Those who would counsel
it join hands with those whose acts have
threatened to destroy the government. There
is no middle ground. Every attempt to prevent
the formation of a new police force is a blow at
the government. That way treason lies. No
man has a right to place his own ease or convenience or the opportunity of making money
above his duty to the State.

"This is the cause of all the people. I call on
every citizen to stand by me in executing the
oath of my office by supporting the authority
of the government and resisting all assaults
upon it."

The effect of these incisive words was to
bring public opinion straight to his support.

It ended the incident of the police strike. There was no further serious effort to obstruct the creation of a new police force. That by this series of occurrences and utterances the political career of Mr. Coolidge had been ended was feared by many. On the contrary, it made him. He was reëlected Governor by an overwhelming vote. His plurality was 125,101. He carried many of the industrial centres. Organized labor did not, as a unit, oppose him. In fact, a large portion of the voters who were members of labor organizations voted for him. No more decisive approval by an electorate of a stand for right has been recorded.

In one of his speeches, years before, Coolidge had said: "Men do not make laws, they but discover them." Of this dramatic chapter in Massachusetts history it might with equal significance be said that the police strike did not make Coolidge, it but revealed him. There is nothing in his official utterances at that time which was not foreshadowed by earlier papers and addresses. The whole structure of his presentation of the issue of the strike was formed from certain convictions relating to government and law which he had set forth on many occasions less acute. The general public, however, and particularly those who lived outside of New England, knew nothing of his earlier addresses, and nothing of his mental attitude or moral perception. The police strike provided a spectacular stage upon which stepped a figure in the fullest glare of publicity, and the country could not but see him. What it saw, it liked.

To say that but for the strike Mr. Coolidge would not have attained national position is idle. We do not know what would have happened; but we may fairly suppose that those qualities which were and are his would have found manifestation sooner or later in some way that would capture the attention of the country.

It has been believed by many students of American affairs that the settlement of the Boston police strike, and more particularly

Governor Coolidge's concise summing up of the
issues involved, had a salutary effect upon the
nation. We are concerned here with the consequences of these incidents upon the personality
of the most conspicuous figure in them; yet in
order to understand fully the rapid expansion
of his fame, and especially if we are to understand why it remained in the public mind so
long, we have to take into account the broadest
results of the affair. These include what may
be fairly called the effect upon the nation —
not simply the immediate effect on Coolidge
as an individual. There was present in many
minds in many parts of the country a sub-
conscious feeling akin to fear; there were disturbing rumblings of an embittered discontent
which many believed presaged disaster. Asser-
tions antagonistic to orderly government had
been made in many places. The authority of
government everywhere in this country was
being questioned or challenged. Those most
sensitive to national psychology were beginning to wonder how law and order could be

restored to that position which they had normally occupied — a position in which it had
never been necessary to defend them, since
they had been taken for granted as the normal
attributes of a representative democracy. The
country had seen an increasing tendency to
flout authority. No way had appeared by
which to turn this drift. It did not suffice to
meet acute crises by a simple show of force.
Such manifestations of authority might serve
to avert a specific catastrophe. They did not
serve either to restore the sense of government's
inviolability or to reassure those who were
fearful for the people. It is not easy to define
precisely the state of mind of the country in
September 1919. There was no specific point
for argument. The feeling of trepidation, like
the feeling of unrest which engendered it, was
vague, undefined, and elusive. This subcon-
scious wish for something to restore confidence
was suddenly, dramatically, and adequately
met by two public documents issued by Governor Coolidge, — the September 14 telegram

to Samuel Gompers, and the September 24 proclamation, — both of which we have fully cited.

The concrete fact was this: the Governor of an American State had asserted, with the full authority of his Commonwealth, and with the overwhelming support of the public, that "the authority of the Commonwealth cannot be intimidated or coerced. It cannot be compromised." He did not argue the case; he stated a truth. In the light of after events it may appear to have been a very simple thing to do. None other had done it. The police strike provided a theatrical situation. Governor Coolidge plucked from it and gave to the American people a vital truth, the obviousness of which had been forgotten.

The increasing feeling of apprehension throughout the country was immediately relieved. The people suddenly saw that the Governor of an American State could and would uphold — even at the risk of his political future — law, order, and government. It was precisely this reassurance for which they had been waiting. Governor Coolidge, and Massachusetts, served the purpose of exemplifying the foundations of a free democracy, able and determined to protect liberty and to forestall licence. Moral and legal responsibility had been dramatically and unequivocally emphasized.

This was a permanent impression on the public mind. In that permanence the reputation of Coolidge shared. That is why the national belief in him did not flag after the close of the incident of the police strike itself. Other men, governors, and statesmen, have met acute crises with courage. What Coolidge did was much more. He restored national confidence in the authority of government. It was inevitable that he should become a national figure, and it was not surprising that he remained one.

He at once became good newspaper "copy." Efforts to interview him were many, and largely unsuccessful. Lacking interviews, writers dug up a wealth of stories emphasizing his brevity of speech and his shrewdness in politics. His Vermont birthplace was invaded by correspondents, and his father and all relatives became celebrated by reflection. He was an unusual type in public life. Many of the stories which have since become familiar were untrue in detail, but most of them faithfully illustrated his peculiarities. Some of them, however, gave a mistaken picture. Those who knew him had not found him hopelessly silent. They knew that he would talk freely and well when the situation called for it. Stories of his thrift gave to some the impression of lack of generosity. These were in error. Mr. Coolidge is not ungenerous. He is not unthoughtful. A man who writes several letters a week to his stepmother, as Mr. Coolidge did until her death in 1920, is a thoughtful son. A man who calls up a newspaper acquaintance, on the latter's return from Plymouth, to ask concerning his stepmother's condition, is not lacking in fine sentiment.

Mr. Coolidge's second term as Governor began in an atmosphere quite different from that of his first. He now had the prestige of national prominence with him. In that fact lay a grave danger to him. He was a national figure. His duty was to be Governor of a State. He was being discussed in terms of national thought. He must proceed on lines of State concern. It is to his credit that he remained essentially and entirely the Governor of Massachusetts. Efforts were made to inveigle him into discussion of national issues. He refused to yield to what might have been a temptation to a less austere man. He was concerned with Massachusetts. Whatever the popular estimate of him, he had been elected to the governorship and to nothing else. His sense of proportion and propriety sustained him. He did not step from the plain pathway of duty. His second term as Governor was marked by exactly the same devotion to the Commonwealth which distinguished his first term.

On election day, November 4, 1919, he

issued a statement to the press, in which he expressed his thanks to the citizens of Massachusetts. In this statement he directed public attention not to anything that he had done, but to what impressed him as the sanity and patriotism of the voters of Massachusetts. "No misrepresentation," he said, "has blinded them, no sophistry has turned them. They listened to the truth and followed it. They have again disappointed those who mistrusted them. They have justified those who trusted them. They have justified America." Thus the emphasis was placed not upon himself, but upon the people. The credit was recognized as theirs. No boastful line appeared in his election day statement. It ended in these words: —

"Three words tell the result: Massachusetts is America. The election will be a welcome demonstration to the nation and to people everywhere who believe that liberty can only be secured by obedience to law."

The temptation to a man under as wide a shower of praise as fell upon him must have been considerable. Many throughout the country believed that they had found a new Moses to lead them out of the wilderness. He would not accept the rôle. That he had ideas on matters of national import is true. That he regarded it as beyond the scope of a State governorship to utter them was equally true. The public might regard him as a figure potent in the larger field; he regarded his duty as well defined and circumscribed by the constitutional limits of his office. There were matters of State importance requiring his attention. To them he devoted all his energies. This was easier for him than it might have been to some other men. To an intense degree he held the governorship of Massachusetts in respect. It has always been to him an office of dignity and of importance, second only to the presidency of the United States. It required no effort on his part to concentrate his abilities and his earnestness upon purely State affairs. Those who sought to lead him elsewhere soon discovered the futility of their efforts. Those who knew him well did not undertake it. It is probable that he simply told himself that as Governor of Massachusetts he had all he could do. It is probable that he dismissed entirely from his thoughts everything except the task in hand. This, until the agitation for his further advancement reached such a stage that he could not further ignore it. The moment when he first came under specific consideration as potentially a candidate for President is marked by another milestone in his career.

The new turn of possibilities, projecting him as of presidential timber, while it necessitated his own recognition of the fact, did not alter his conduct of his office. Throughout the difficult period when his friends were preparing a campaign in his behalf he remained the Governor. Probably few campaigns in behalf of a man for so high honor have received so little assistance from the proposed candidate. If Mr. Coolidge had any interest in the plans of his friends at this time he gave scant evidence of it. He was hardly approachable on this topic. Callers at his office who sought to lead him into discussion of his own political future met no encouragement. Either they talked State affairs, or their call was soon ended. The Governor's office in the Massachusetts State House did not become a political headquarters. The two-room apartment in the Adams House occupied by Mr. and Mrs. Coolidge remained simply their home and did not become the scene of a political adventure.

The police strike had materially altered the public attitude toward Calvin Coolidge; it had not altered him. He was exactly the same man in January 1920 that he had been in January 1919, plus the advantage of one year's experience as Chief Executive of a State. His views on principles of government and law were precisely the same. His conception of his duty as a public man had not been changed. However dramatic the police strike may have been in the view of the public, it was to him apparently one item in the day's work.

It was this cool, self-possessed, serious and silent man who was soon forced by events into the national arena.

VII

A NATIONAL FIGURE: NOMINATED
FOR VICE-PRESIDENT

THE apparent hopelessness of nominating for President of the United States a resident of Massachusetts might have daunted less earnest champions than those who now undertook development of Governor Coolidge in such a rôle. The effort to make a similar nomination in a Republican National Convention had been made a few years previously and, though the candidate was a statesman of the first rank, the effort failed. It seems astonishing, in view of the geographical handicap, that it should have been seriously proposed to nominate Coolidge for President in 1920. Yet the fact is that, as soon as the movement was started, it found a highly favorable reception in many parts of the country far distant from New England. This was because the sentiment of the

American people had been deeply stirred by the demonstration in Massachusetts of a sound principle, and by the crystallization of that principle and its effective application by this man. Mr. Coolidge was discovered to be, in the national mind, a personification of something which the public enthusiastically approved.

To locate the precise beginning — so far as public thought was concerned — of the Coolidge candidacy is not possible. Probably the first newspaper mention of a specific nature suggesting him as a candidate was in a Boston evening newspaper shortly following the police strike. This, of course, was not the origin of the idea. It is commonly and correctly understood that his best friend, Frank W. Stearns, saw in him, when he was a member of the State Senate, qualities which he believed equipped him to be President of the country. Such fore-vision in politics is not common. That Coolidge's fame — due to the police strike — was shrewdly capitalized is the fact. A volume containing specimens of his public papers and addresses had nation-wide circulation. They strengthened public approval of the man. They revealed him. If the police strike served as an advertisement, those who were partially persuaded by it were satisfied with the goods upon examination. The picture of Coolidge was one of a man possessed of common sense, a capacity to state truths clearly, and a refreshing disinclination to waste words. His understanding of American government appeared to be in concise accord with what the bulk of the American people believed. His second inaugural address, delivered January 9, 1920, had attracted a degree of attention commensurate with his fame. In it, many for the first time found expressed one of the foundation beliefs of Coolidge concerning efficient democracy. "In general," he said, "it is a time to conserve, to retrench rather than to reform; a time to stabilize the administration of the present laws rather than to seek new legislation."

In this address also he made a plea for the

"humanizing" of industry. This plea he closed
with the words : "Change not the law, but the
attitude of the mind."

There was nothing in this inaugural address
to indicate that he was cherishing thoughts of
personal ambition. He continued his concentration upon State affairs. His friends were not
similarly inactive in the larger field. His mail
was heavy. From all parts of the country letters came to him praising his stand in the police
strike, and many of them approved the plan to
make him a candidate of the Republican party
for President. The Republican Club of Massachusetts issued a formal endorsement of his
candidacy. From other States came tentative
overtures favoring his nomination for Vice-
President. To all of these letters, resolutions,
and encouragements Mr. Coolidge remained
uniformly noncommittal. The movement for
his nomination continued without his consent
or coöperation.

He had received from President Wilson a
telegram offering congratulations upon his

reëlection. This further emphasized the idea that he had done something quite beyond the fields of political partisanship. His position at the beginning of the campaign in his behalf was unusual, if not unique.

Meantime this campaign had become organized. James B. Reynolds, who had served notably as Secretary of the Republican National Committee, severed his connection with that committee and was placed in charge of the campaign in New England. His headquarters were at the Parker House in Boston. Correspondence passed between these headquarters and all parts of the country. Probably a similar campaign was never conducted. Governor Coolidge personally had no part in it. To undertake the nomination of a man who will not even discuss it, presents difficulties.

At this same time the candidacy of General Leonard Wood was receiving strong impetus throughout the country. He also had the status of a Massachusetts candidate. It became evident that in the election of delegates to the Republican National Convention some, perhaps many, would be either pledged to, or inclined toward, the nomination of Wood. In this situation Governor Coolidge issued a remarkable political statement. It was without precedent. It placed his supporters in a difficult position; but it increased the respect in which he was held. This statement, issued in January 1920, shortly after his inauguration as Governor, was as follows: —

"The times require of men charged with public responsibility a singleness of purpose. The curse of the present is the almost universal grasping for power in high places and in low, to the exclusion of the discharge of obligations. It is always well for men to walk humbly.

"The great office of Governor of the Commonwealth of Massachusetts has twice been conferred upon me. There is no higher honor in the gift of her people. There is only one higher honor in the gift of the people of the nation. For that office my name has been proposed by men whose judgment entitles their decisions to a great respect, and their proposal has not been unsupported by a most respectable public approval. For all this I am deeply appreciative, with an appreciation which words alone cannot express. There must be acts to correspond.

"I have never said I will become a candidate for President. I have never accepted, unless by silence, efforts made by statesmen of more than national reputation to present my name to the Convention. I have made it plain I could not seek this office.

"Some weeks ago it was represented to me that certain forces in Massachusetts desired to support me. No contest for delegates has ever been contemplated. I have no purpose to enter such a contest. The probable outcome of a contest needs not to be considered at all. It is enough to know that some Massachusetts people intend to make one. The question is whether I ought to permit a contest in my name for delegates in my own State.

"I have taken no position in which I need

to withdraw. I do not wish to embarrass anyone. I have a great desire to walk humbly and
discharge my obligations. My paramount obligation is not to expose the great office of Governor, but to guard and protect it. The people
are entitled to know that their office is to be
administered not for my benefit, but for their
benefit, and that I am not placing myself in any
position where any other object could be inferred. There must be no imputation, however
unfounded, that I permit their office to be used
anywhere for manipulated purposes. I cannot
consent to have their office taken into any contest for delegates in my own State. I have not
been and I am not a candidate for President.

"I do not pretend to be insensible to the
high honor that the mention of my name has
brought me. The support of the people has
touched me. For all this I am not lacking in
gratitude.

"But the great fact remains that it is a time
to counsel not with desire, but with duty. My
duty, clear, plain, unequivocal, is to the people

of Massachusetts. To Massachusetts, unafraid, orderly, patriotic, American, in the discharge of every duty an example to the nation."

The sincerity of that statement has never been and cannot be questioned. It rang true. It was absolutely consistent with everything in his career. It accorded with his words and with his acts. "Do the day's work" has been called the Coolidge motto. Certainly we find, in analyzing his motives from the evidence of his acts and words, that it was both his principle and his custom to give undivided attention to the task in hand. What might have been the result had Mr. Coolidge undertaken personal leadership or prominence in a contest for delegates, no man knows. In his statement he observed truly that the probable outcome of such a contest needed not to be considered.

Once again Mr. Coolidge had stated the meat of an issue so clearly that none mistook it. The issue was not the material one of whether or not he could obtain a delegation pledged to his support. The issue was one involving the obligations in an office to which he had just been elected by the voters of his State. His vision of his duty was clear, and it was exactly what might have been expected from knowledge of his career.

Speculation as to the political adroitness of the statement is not permissible, because to undertake it would be to dilute the sincerity of the statement itself. This none would do. Yet in the light of subsequent events it is clear that Mr. Coolidge's standing in the mind of the nation was further enhanced. Once again he had presented to the country a picture that it liked. He added nothing new to the picture already familiar, but he clinched its truth. That this statement did seriously embarrass his campaign-managers is true. On the day of its issuance and before its publication, one of the men closest to Mr. Coolidge, accompanied by a friend, made a hurried call at the Governor's living-quarters at the Adams House. The purpose of the visit was to persuade the Governor, if possible, to make a very slight alteration in this statement. Principally, it was desired to insert one word in one sentence. The word was "active." The sentence would then read, "I have not been and I am not an active candidate for President." This would have left his campaign committee, now very much adrift, free to pursue a charted course. The conversation in the Governor's hotel room went something like this : —

"You have given your statement to the press?"

"Yes."

"Is it too late to call it back?"

"No."

"Are you willing to call it back?"

"No."

"Governor, we want to make one very slight change. We want to insert the word 'active.' This will leave your friends in a position where they can do something. As it is, we don't know what to do. Will you consent to this change?"

"No; statement stands."

Mr. Coolidge would not change his statement so much as by a comma. It appeared in the newspapers exactly as he had written it. This was one occasion in which he had gone over the heads of his friends and advisers. He chose his own way. He would not modify it in any respect. The statement stood.

Nevertheless, the campaign in his behalf continued, with this modification: there was of course no contest for delegates. It was believed that if unpledged delegates were sent to Chicago they could feel free to vote for the nomination of Coolidge without his consent. The propriety of such a course was unquestioned. The result was the election of delegates, some of whom were favorable to the nomination of Coolidge and some to the nomination of Leonard Wood. Thus the Massachusetts delegation was a unit for no candidate. This, it may be observed, was not without precedent in Massachusetts politics.

During all the discussion of the Coolidge candidacy, Winthrop Murray Crane, former

Senator and former Governor, had been sympathetic and encouraging. Mr. Crane's attention had been drawn to Coolidge several years earlier. They became close political friends. That Mr. Coolidge profited from the wise counsel of Mr. Crane is true. Mr. Crane saw in him the making of a brilliant future and to the achievement of this he lent his aid. That the two men consulted frequently in matters of State policy was well known. Mr. Crane's long experience and profound knowledge in all matters relating to State and national affairs were always at the command of Mr. Coolidge as Governor. That he availed himself of these advantages indicates his sagacity. When the movement for his nomination to the presidency began, Mr. Crane coöperated. Throughout that movement his counsel was frequently summoned and always sympathetically given to Mr. Coolidge's supporters. All that he legitimately could do to advance the Coolidge candidacy at the National Convention, he did. Much of Coolidge's political training in the half dozen years of his career preceding Mr. Crane's death he received from this quarter. Mr. Crane was his chief political adviser.

Warren G. Harding, United States Senator from Ohio, was nominated for President by the Republican party on the tenth ballot of the 1920 convention in Chicago. Mr. Coolidge's name figured in each of these ballots, but at no time was he within striking distance of the nomination. The chance that he might be chosen rested upon the fact that a deadlock occurred among the three leading candidates. In escaping from that deadlock, a so-called "dark horse" must be chosen. Among these possibilities was Coolidge. His friends hoped that at the proper moment a sufficient number of votes in his favor could be shown to start among the delegates a winning movement to nominate him. In fact, his campaign had been constructed largely with the understanding that such a deadlock would occur. The same Boston evening newspaper which supported him throughout prophesied this deadlock precisely as it occurred. Warren Harding, not Calvin Coolidge, was chosen to break the deadlock. On no ballot in the convention did Coolidge have an united Massachusetts delegation. On the first ballot Coolidge received 29 votes. Of these 28 came from the thirty-five Massachusetts delegates. The other vote was cast by T. M. Reed of Nome, who was the delegate from Alaska. He voted for Coolidge because he had been impressed by his attitude in the police strike, and by his book, *Have Faith in Massachusetts*. The other seven Massachusetts votes on this ballot were given to General Wood.

On the second ballot Massachusetts voted as on the first. The total Coolidge vote on this ballot was 32. This was his maximum vote during the Convention. On the next ballot Coolidge received 21 votes from Massachusetts and 6 from other sources. On the fourth ballot Coolidge lost 2 votes from his own State, retaining the other 6. On the fifth ballot he received 22 from Massachusetts and 7 from elsewhere. Wood on this ballot received 13 Massachusetts votes. The Massachusetts delegation thenceforth, until the tenth and final ballot, showed little change. Coolidge's total Convention vote was, on the sixth ballot, 28; on the seventh, 23; on the eighth, 30; on the ninth, 28, and on the tenth, 5. On this ballot the Massachusetts delegation voted as follows: Harding, 17; Wood, 17; Coolidge, 1. One member only of the Massachusetts delegation voted for Coolidge on each of the ten ballots. He was William Whiting of Holyoke. Whether Mr. Coolidge's position before the Convention would have been politically more effective had he taken a personal interest in strengthening it, is doubtful. It is probably true that his position throughout was not only ethically correct but politically sound. He had been urged to be present at the Convention. He flatly declined to do so. He reiterated informally, not in any political statement, that his work was as Governor of Massachusetts, and that he had neither the time nor the

willingness to do anything else. While friends
were working in his behalf at the Chicago
Convention, Governor Coolidge was at his
office in the Massachusetts State House. He
would not discuss the Chicago situation.

The Coolidge headquarters occupied two
rooms in the Congress Hotel in Chicago. Most
of the candidates' gathering-places were at
this hotel, excepting that of Hiram Johnson,
who was established across the street, in
the Auditorium. In all of these personal headquarters the candidate was in evidence, with
the single exception of Mr. Coolidge. There
was no splurge or brass band connected with
his candidacy. The campaign material most
circulated in his behalf in Chicago was a re-
print of his own speeches and writings.

The number of votes cast for Coolidge in the
Convention did not indicate his strength. That
he was under serious consideration by many of
the delegates who did not vote for him was
known to his supporters. It was this latent
strength, for which no occasion provided the

opportunity for demonstration in votes in the ten ballots, which finally gave him the nomination for Vice-President. That nomination is one of the striking things in the history of Republican party politics. It is a curious fact that, although Mr. Coolidge's personality is the reverse of sensational, many events in his public career have been dramatic. Such was his nomination for Vice-President. With Senator Harding nominated for the head of the ticket, Convention interest lagged. It was tacitly understood around the Convention hall, among delegates and onlookers, that the vice-presidential nominee would be Senator Irvine L. Lenroot of Wisconsin. So little interest was being taken in the approaching ballot for Vice-President that many of the delegates had left the Convention hall. The absentees included a large portion of the Massachusetts delegation. Judge McCamant, of Portland, Oregon, arose and was recognized by the Chairman of the Convention. To the unqualified surprise of nearly everyone present, he proposed the name of Governor Coolidge for Vice-President. Within thirty seconds it was plain that the nomination would be so made. During the voting on the names of candidates for the head of the ticket there had been the usual demonstrations, in which the galleries joined and even appeared in some instances to lead. These demonstrations were well organized. There had been no spontaneous enthusiasm among the delegates themselves, even when Senator Harding was finally nominated. That nomination was heartily cheered under the leadership of the Ohio delegation, with the usual parade of delegates up and down the aisles. To those familiar with political conventions these occasions of applause were the usual and accustomed thing, somewhat accelerated by conscious effort.

The outburst of enthusiasm which followed Judge McCamant's mention of the name of Coolidge was of a different sort. It sprang immediately and boisterously from the delegates in all parts of the hall. A veteran newspaper correspondent turned to his neighbor in the press enclosure and said, "It's all over. Coolidge is nominated." This was the fact. On the first ballot Mr. Coolidge received 674½ votes; Lenroot received 146½.

It has been said that the Convention supposed, when Judge McCamant rose, that he did so for the purpose of seconding the nomination of Lenroot, which had already been made. It is immaterial whether this is so or not. Had Judge McCamant not nominated Coolidge, someone else would have. Credit must be given the Oregon man for a brief but eloquent and effective nominating speech; that it touched off the enthusiasm of the delegates is undeniable. But the voting for Coolidge was on the merits of his candidacy. As soon as the event had occurred, it became clear to everyone in the hall that the nomination of Coolidge for second place, he having missed first place, was inevitable.

It has been asked why that enthusiasm which carried Coolidge into the vice-presidential nomination could not have been stirred in his behalf in the earlier instance of balloting for President. Conditions were not the same. The nominating speech and its seconding in the presidential balloting had been good. Coolidge was nominated as a candidate for President by Frederick H. Gillett, Speaker of the National House of Representatives. To the authority of his office Mr. Gillett brought a discreet eloquence. His speech was in good taste. It probably could not have been improved upon. The nomination was seconded by Mrs. Alexandra Carlisle Pfeiffer, who had been sent as an alternate delegate to the Convention. Her stage training and attractive personality, and the unusualness of a woman appearing in such a rôle, had united to maintain the Convention's good opinion of the Coolidge cause. Whether any different nominating speech could have made Coolidge the candidate for President may be doubted. The psychological position of the delegates at the end of an exhausting week, and with the nomination of a presidential candidate disposed of, was one in which mention of the name of Coolidge fitted precisely. The delegates were in a condition of nervous tension, awaiting a chance for relief. They had carried in their minds always a friendly feeling toward Coolidge. Mention of his name by Judge McCamant set free the emotional reaction of these men. The nomination followed.

There is one particularly striking sentence in Judge McCamant's nominating speech. It is this: "He is big enough and sound enough to be President of the United States, should occasion require." Which brings us back to a thought expressed many pages back: that the nomination of Calvin Coolidge for Vice-President differed from many nominations made for that office in the fact that those who nominated him had throughout the Convention had in their minds a picture of him as a potential President. This consideration has a personal as well as a general political significance. Throughout his political career Mr. Coolidge has been called "different." He himself would be unable to explain this. His nomination as a candidate for national office was based upon this quality of being "different." It is inexact to say that he owes his nomination to the Boston police strike. He owes his nomination to qualities in him which the police strike revealed to the people of the country.

VIII

VICE–PRESIDENT AND PRESIDENT

It was characteristic of Governor Coolidge that neither his nomination nor his election to the vice-presidency altered in the slightest degree his attitude toward the office to which he had been elected in November 1919. He continued to perform the duties of Governor as if his name had never gone before the National Convention of his party. He had been elected to that office — he proposed to see it through. He had been inaugurated in January 1920. His term was to expire in January 1921. He was to become Vice-President March 4, 1921. He felt that he had time to do in Massachusetts what he had been elected by its citizens to do, and that he had time for nothing else. When, some time subsequent to his nomination, he was asked why he did not take a long vacation, he said he had no time.

"Mr. Harding is going to take a rest," he was told. "Mr. Harding," said Governor Coolidge, "is not Governor of Massachusetts."

The formal notification to Coolidge of his nomination took place July 27, 1920, at an open-air gathering on the recreation grounds of Smith College, at Northampton. The speech was delivered by Governor Morrow of Kentucky. To this speech Mr. Coolidge made a brief reply. The scene was one of rare beauty. The sloping lawns of the Smith College campus provided a setting finely typical of American democracy; the crowd was not essentially a political gathering. It had more the appearance of a coming-together of the neighbors. It was like an open-air party, with music by a brass band, and it was difficult to see in it the serious significance that really was there. Mrs. Coolidge of course was with her husband; and his father, Colonel John Coolidge, also. When the ceremony was ended, and the crowd had gathered in little family groups, a friend of the Coolidges came upon Colonel John, standing by himself. "This

must be a great day for your family, Colonel,"
he said. "We are all very proud of your son,
and we expect great things from him." The
father's comment was characteristically conservative. It was this:—

"I hope you 'll never be disappointed."

The Coolidges do not "slop over." After
Calvin had become President, someone made
to his father a similar expression of confidence
in the son. "Well," said the Colonel, "Calvin
made a fair Governor, and I guess he 'll make
a fair President."

A friend at the Northampton affair stopped
to speak to Mrs. Coolidge as she was about to
leave the grounds. "I suppose," he said, "that
you will both take a little rest now. This
must have been a tiring day for both of you."

Mrs. Coolidge laughed: "Calvin says it is
about like any other day. We are going right
back to Boston."

Governor Coolidge was at his desk at the
State House at the usual hour, next morning.

An event occurred early in the fall which

must be chronicled. On October 2, 1920, Winthrop Murray Crane died at his home in Dalton. He was sixty-seven years old. The association between Mr. Crane and Mr. Coolidge had been close and mutually advantageous. It is one of the tragedies of politics, and of life, that he should have died before his friend entered upon his duties as Vice-President.

Mr. Coolidge as candidate for second place on the ticket did not usurp any of the attention which normally should go to the candidate for President. He made a number of speeches in which he expressed general views on government with which his friends were familiar. In October he, in company with Frank A. Lowden of Illinois, Job E. Hedges of New York, Governor Morrow of Kentucky, and others, made an interesting campaign trip through Kentucky, Tennessee, North Carolina, Virginia, West Virginia, and Maryland. This was an invasion of Democratic territory. He was well received, and it has been judged that the trip was wise. Mr. Coolidge's speeches included eight or ten prepared addresses, delivered to considerable gatherings. Perhaps more important were the ten-minute speeches which he made from the rear platform of the special train which was provided and financed by the Republican National Committee. This train-end speaking was a new experience to Governor Coolidge. During the first evening of the trip a newspaperman sitting with the Governor in the drawing-room car, asked him how he looked forward to the week. "I don't like it," he said. "I don't like to speak. It's all nonsense. I'd much better be at home doing my work."

Nevertheless, his distaste for speaking was considerably modified before the week was ended. The experience of standing on the rear platform of the train and talking to hastily gathered groups of men and women in the mountain regions of the border states stirred in him a new understanding of the people whose Vice-President he was presumably soon to become. There is no question that this trip impressed him and added to his comprehension of the nation. These informal speeches were thoroughly successful.

In November Mr. Harding was elected President and Mr. Coolidge Vice-President by a very large plurality. Mr. Coolidge continued his business as Governor of Massachusetts without interruption.

One of the interesting items in the campaign, the consequences of which are now far better comprehended than they were when in the stage of discussion, was Mr. Harding's proposal that the Vice-President should have a seat at the Cabinet meetings. The plan had public approval. We must suppose that this was less because of any principle involved than because of that peculiar quality of the Coolidge candidacy to which reference was made in the last chapter. Mr. Coolidge occupied a position in the public mind which made his chief's suggestion welcome. It was felt that his counsel would be useful to Mr. Harding, and that Mr. Harding showed a fine consideration in making the suggestion. While not without precedent, the plan was unusual. President Taft had invited Vice-President Sherman to his Cabinet meetings.

Possibilities of confusion must accompany any such procedure. Except in the event of the death of a President, the Vice-President's duties consist of presiding over the United States Senate. In the Senate he has no vote except in the event of a tie, in which he may cast the deciding ballot. He thus occupies a position of intimate association with the chief legislative body of the nation. To sit in the meetings of the Cabinet, he must assume a position highly confidential in the executive branch. The distinction between the legislative and executive branches of our government has always been kept clear. To make the Vice-President a confidant of both branches suggests an obvious peril. It is evidence of Mr. Harding's confidence in Mr. Coolidge that he proposed this course. It is evidence of Mr. Coolidge's tact, good taste, and sanity that he acted under that suggestion without arousing the slightest criticism from either the executive or the legislative leaders.

The vice-presidency had been regarded as a political morgue. Theodore Roosevelt had proved that it is not necessarily so. The peculiar circumstances under which Mr. Coolidge had been elected to the office, and the series of achievements in his record before election, had led to a rather vague expectation that he would not fall into political oblivion in Washington. As a matter of fact, he did. This was no fault of his own, yet it accorded probably very closely with his own expectations. He had never sought self-advertisement. He had been advertised by events. Events do not occur to advertise a Vice-President. He did some public speaking; in these speeches he did little more than to echo the Administration, that is to say, President Harding. This was consistent with his record. It will be recalled that in his campaign for the lieutenant-governorship of Massachusetts, and subsequently in that office, he restricted his utterances within limits of the strictest loyalty to his chief. This was precisely his course as Vice-President. After the novelty of his personality had worn off, Washington newspaper correspondents found him "poor copy." He was approachable, but he had little to say.

On the occasion of his first appearance at a Cabinet meeting he was met by newspapermen as he left the White House. They asked him what seat he occupied. His reply was to the effect that any such information must come from the President. This was an extreme of caution, because a photographer had taken a picture of the meeting which of course showed where Coolidge sat. The incident served, however, to discourage interviewers. After a time the newspapermen forgot him, excepting those representing New England papers. They found him valuable for consultation, but not productive of news. The obscurity which enshrouds the personality of a Vice-President captured him as most of his predecessors.

He presided over the Senate ably and without partisanship. His conception of the office was not that of a man elected on a party ticket, but as the impersonal presiding officer of a great legislative body. His rulings were rarely challenged, and more rarely upset. He played no politics from the chair. Personal friendship obtained no advantage for any Senator seeking the privilege of the floor. Democrats found no difficulty in obtaining recognition. He frequently called Democrats to the chair to take his place during his absence in the lunch hour. Mr. Pomerene of Ohio, who before his defeat in November 1922 was a serious possibility for the Democratic nomination for President, sometimes presided over the Senate. So did Senator Joseph T. Robinson of Arkansas, who in the Sixty-eighth Congress succeeds Senator Underwood as minority floor-leader. Democrats who might be expected to attack the Republicans were given full opportunity to do so. In short, presiding officer Coolidge gave full play to that free speech for which the Senate has been always notable. He presided with dignity. There never was anything flippant or trivial in his manner. Perhaps it may be stated here that a story circulated during his first year in office regarding his New England accent was, happily, incorrect. The story was that an operation on his nasal passages had destroyed that celebrated Vermont method of speech for which he had been famous. The public may be assured that he speaks as nasally as always. He still can pronounce "cow" with four syllables.

Mr. Coolidge took his duties as Vice-President precisely as he had taken other duties. He did the day's work. He did not seek publicity. That he kept informed in all national matters may have escaped the attention of the newspapermen who chose to forget him, but it was well understood by those who knew him best. Many of his friends called on him in the Vice-President's office at the Capitol, at his rooms in the Senate Office Building, or at the New Willard Hotel where he lived.

No man in Washington public life during the period of his vice-presidency was better informed as to political events or concerning the personalities and motives of members of the Senate. Whether the Senators realized that their presiding officer was studying them each and individually may be doubted; his friends knew it to be so. He knew what each Senator would be likely to say or do. This applied to both parties. Few men have had a more accurate understanding of the United States Senate than the man who presided over it from March 4, 1921, until the death of President Harding.

The drama of the police strike had first directed the nation's thought to Coolidge. The tragedy of a President's death brought him back into the public mind. On August 2, 1923, President Harding died. Before dawn, August 3, Calvin Coolidge took the oath of office and became President. The oath was administered by his father, as a justice of the peace, in the family sitting-room at Plymouth, Vermont. It was a scene of the utmost simplicity. Light was furnished by a kerosene lamp. Mr. Coolidge, now President, rested two or three hours, then hurried at once to Washington.

There followed an immediate revival of interest in the man who had so captured the country's fancy in 1920. Confidence in Mr. Coolidge manifested itself at once. He remained the same man, unchanged by events. Twenty-four hours earlier he had been out of the public mind; now the eyes of all the world were upon him. The magic of circumstance was operating. He made a satisfying impression. He took over the reins of responsibility with dignity and self-respect. He made no grandiloquent speech. He was a modest man accepting his duty. The country liked him and what he did. His prompt decision to retain intact the machinery of administration organized by his predecessor was approved. Rumors went broadcast of impending changes in the Cabinet. There were none. A temporary White House was established at the New Willard Hotel. It swarmed with political leaders and newspapermen. There was a constant procession of official callers upon the new President. They entered expectant; most of them came forth mystified. One of the rumors was that Attorney-General Daugherty would resign; he had been President Harding's closest political adviser. He called upon President Coolidge. When he came out from the audience newspapermen crowded about him. "What did you talk about?" they asked. "Why," said Mr. Daugherty, "we talked about — er — railroads." "Was anything said about the resignation?" "Whose resignation?" asked Daugherty, and he departed. That was the substance of most of the newspapermen's efforts to get information from those who called on the new President. These callers had no information to give out — because, presumably, they had learned nothing. President Coolidge was not communicative. He was conducting the presidency much as he had conducted the governorship of Massachusetts.

A Massachusetts friend called upon President Coolidge. "Just think," he said, "five years ago you were just a Lieutenant-Governor of Massachusetts. Now you are the most powerful man in the world."

"Well," said the President, "I don't think of it that way."

"You are; and you know you are."

"There may be something to it."

That is an accurate picture of Mr. Coolidge's attitude. In his statement of January 1920, insisting that he was not a candidate for the presidential nomination, he had expressed a desire to walk humbly. He is walking humbly. Exaltation of office has not changed him.

One by one the rumors of drastic changes in Washington faded away. No changes of importance were made. The machinery of administration continued, with only that pause of respect and sorrow involved in the burial of a President who had died at his post of duty. Throughout this period of mourning the new President, Mr. Coolidge, effaced himself as much as possible. His course was marked by discretion, courtesy, and reverence for the memory of his Chief.

An immediate problem was before him. A strike impended in the Pennsylvania anthracite regions. What would President Coolidge do? He followed his habitual custom of proceeding in precise conformity with what existing laws and authority indicated. The mines were operated under and regulated by Pennsylvania State laws. He conferred with the Governor of that State. The Governor effected a settlement. The menace of a strike was lifted.

Pressure was brought to bear to induce the President to summon the Sixty-eighth Congress in special session. This pressure he resisted as his predecessor had.

Mr. and Mrs. Coolidge moved into the White House. Their two sons remained at work; one in a western Massachusetts tobacco-field, the other in the training camp at Devens. There was no ostentation about Mr. Coolidge's taking his new position. The feverish efforts of writers to find texts for news stories began to dwindle. The Government had settled down to prosaic business. There was to be no more drama. Mr. Coolidge picked up the reins fallen from the hands of Mr. Harding. The routine of national administration was resumed. Holders of office discovered that they were secure. Mr. Coolidge made no announcement of policies. It became understood that such announcement should in propriety be made to Congress, soon to assemble.

Meantime, President Coolidge was the man his friends had always known—quiet, business-like, modest, and sure.

IX

LOOKING FORWARD

CALVIN COOLIDGE's permanent place in history is yet to be determined. Immediately upon his taking the oath of office he became what is known as the "logical" candidate for nomination in 1924. This, because it is political logic to renominate the Administration unless there are circumstances making it impossible or patently inadvisable. President Harding would have been renominated had he lived. President Coolidge now became the personification of the Republican Administration. Selection of him as the candidate in 1924 would not be a renomination for him, but a nomination; he has not yet been nominated for that office and therefore could not be renominated. Such a selection, however, would be a renomination of the Republican Administration. President Coolidge inherited the assets, responsibilities, and opportunities of the Harding régime. He escaped its embarrassments. His decision to retain practically intact the administrative machinery assembled by Harding showed good executive judgment; it is to be gauged by that measure. It was also good politics.

Prophecies looking six months ahead in politics are hazardous. No one can foresee what will occur in a convention whose personnel and issues are likely to be determined by events the nature of which is as yet unrevealed. The quick assumption was made that by virtue of his accession to the office he would be his party's candidate in the next election. His first acts as President were measured from that point of view.

The first important appointment he made was immediately interpreted by the critical as a move in the direction of controlling the next National Convention. He appointed Campbell Bascom Slemp, a former national Representative from Virginia, as Secretary to the President. Virginia is not a Republican State; but the Republican party cherishes fond hopes of penetrating some of the Southern States. Party necessity points in that direction. Defections from the party in districts influenced by the Non-Partisan League and the Farmer-Labor group point with pitiless force the advisability of making gains in other regions. Some of the Southern States had shown vigorous Republican gains in recent years. Many professed to see in the Slemp appointment a personal appeal by Coolidge as a potential candidate for Southern delegates. A more creditable explanation is available. Every President needs political advice. Every President needs a medium of contact with both branches of Congress. President Coolidge knows the Senate through his association with it as presiding officer. He had to acquire an intimate understanding of the House of Representatives. Mr. Slemp had served prominently in the House. He is an experienced politician. Mr. Coolidge, in appointing him as his executive Secretary, was following a course similar to that taken by nearly all Presidents.

He obtained means of daily consultation with a trained man who, first, knew the House of Representatives; second, knew the intricate ways of politics; third, had a personal understanding of the status of the Republican party in the South. If we are to continue to judge Coolidge as President on the basis of his record in other offices, we have to reject that interpretation of the Slemp appointment which associates it with alleged personal ambitions of Mr. Coolidge. He has never played politics that way.

Presidential nominations are not made without cause. Reasons for a nomination of Coolidge in 1924 consisted — preceding the assembling of the Sixty-eighth Congress — of his achievements in State office. His experience as Vice-President and President of the national Senate had broadened his outlook and increased the scope of his statesmanship, but it contributed little to his qualifications as a candidate for the presidency. In the public mind he represented other things of other years. He still represented the Boston police strike and the stimulating political philosophy which he had uttered in connection with it; he represented also a picture of plain common-sense Americanism. The public attitude toward Coolidge was still friendly. It was more than this. It was expectant. Coolidge was "different." Did he work miracles? The Republican party, which faced many difficulties, believed it had in Coolidge a man to inspire that degree of confidence without which it could not win the next election.

Such being the status of Coolidge, as President and as a potential candidate, during the period between his taking the oath of office and the convening of Congress in December 1923, it is beyond that latter date that danger and opportunity await him. It is foreseen to be a difficult Congress: party discipline is presumed to be lacking, group legislation pressing to the front. President Coolidge faces a dual task: one concerning administration, the other concerning politics. The purely administrative difficulty is similar in principle to problems he has faced in Massachusetts. The political trouble is more intricate. Disregarding the unwarranted assumption that he would chart his course with the gratification of personal ambition as the objective, we know from his record of devotion to the Republican party that he must keep constantly in mind the welfare of that party in carrying the burden of government by his guidance.

However conscientious Mr. Coolidge may be regarding his own political fortunes, to his party he has embodied a new chance. Considerations of party procedure have had nothing whatever to do with personal friendliness or past associations. With the party in a process of closing ranks, in the fall of 1923, just one possible leadership is in sight — the leadership of President Coolidge. That gone, chaos threatens. The necessities of the situation have drawn into assertive support of Mr. Coolidge many who hitherto had regarded him with indifference. Power has made him mighty.

A severe test comes with the convening of Congress. Then Mr. Coolidge must formulate and express his policy as the party's policy. Upon his programme and upon his agility during the Congressional session, and upon his capacity for leadership under most difficult conditions depend his continuing control.

Calvin Coolidge's ascent has been methodical. He has fulfilled every duty as it came to him. He has a sane political philosophy. If the future is to be judged by the past, his friends are justified in their expectations. He faces, as President, vaster problems than he has known before. He stands upon a sure foundation of character. He commands public trust by virtue of the accuracy with which he represents American qualities.

He is of material from which great things may come. Events will try him.

ADDRESS AT THE EXERCISES ON THE
300th ANNIVERSARY OF THE LANDING
OF THE PILGRIMS, AT PLYMOUTH,
MASSACHUSETTS, DECEMBER 21, 1920, BY
CALVIN COOLIDGE, VICE-PRESIDENT ELECT

Plymouth Rock does was not mark a beginning or an end. It marks a revelation of that which is without beginning and without end. It marks a purpose, shining through eternity forth with a resplendent light, undimmed even by the imperfections of men, and a response an answering purpose from those obscure, disdainful of all else, who sought and found an avenue for the immortal soul

THE PILGRIMS

THREE centuries ago to-day the Pilgrims of the "May-flower" made final landing at Plymouth Rock. They came not merely from the shores of the Old World. It will be in vain to search among recorded maps and history for their origin. They sailed up out of the infinite.

There was among them small trace of the vanities of life. They came undecked with orders of nobility. They were not children of fortune but of tribulation. Persecution, not preference, brought them hither; but it was a persecution in which they found a stern satisfaction. They cared little for titles, still less for the goods of this earth, but for an idea they would die. Measured by the standards of men of their time they were the humble of the earth. Measured by later accomplishments they were the mighty. In appearance weak and persecuted they came — rejected, despised, an insignificant band; in reality, strong and independent, a mighty host, of whom the world was not worthy, destined to free mankind. No captain ever led his forces to such a conquest. Oblivious to rank, yet men trace to them their lineage as to a royal house.

Forces not ruled by man had laid their unwilling course. As they landed, a sentinel of Providence, humbler, nearer to nature than themselves, welcomed them in their own tongue. They came seeking only an abiding place on earth, "but lifted up their eyes to heaven, their dearest country," says Governor Bradford, "where God hath prepared for them a city." On that abiding faith has been reared an empire magnificent beyond their dreams of Paradise.

Amid the solitude they set up hearthstone and altar; the home and the church. With arms in their hands they wrung from the soil their bread. With arms they gathered in the congregation to worship Almighty God. But they were armed, that in peace they might seek divine guidance in righteousness; not that they might prevail by force, but that they might do right though they perished.

What an increase, material and spiritual, three hundred years has brought that little company is known to all the earth. No like body ever cast so great an influence on human history. Civilization has made of their landing-place a shrine. Unto the Commonwealth of Massachusetts has been entrusted the keeping of that shrine. To her has come the precious heritage. It will be kept as it was created, or it will perish, not with an earthly pride but with a heavenly vision.

Plymouth Rock does not mark a beginning or an end. It marks a revelation of that which is without beginning and without end — a purpose, shining through eternity with a resplendent light, undimmed even by the imperfections of men; and a response, an answering purpose, from those who, oblivious, disdainful of all else, sailed hither seeking only for an avenue for the immortal soul.